THE
5 AM
MIRACLE

THE
5 AM
MIRACLE

DOMINATE YOUR DAY BEFORE BREAKFAST

JEFF SANDERS

Ulysses Press

Published in the U.S. by
Ulysses Press
P.O. Box 3440
Berkeley, CA 94703
www.ulyssespress.com

ISBN: 978-1-61243-500-8
Library of Congress Control Number: 2015937556

Printed in Canada by Marquis Book Printing

10 9 8 7 6 5 4 3 2

Acquisitions Editor: Kelly Reed
Managing Editor: Claire Chun
Editor: Renee Rutledge
Proofreader: Nancy Bell
Cover design: what!design @ whatweb.com
Cover photo: Tyler Ring
Interior design: Jake Flaherty

Distributed by Publishers Group West

*To my lovely wife, Tessa, and our quirky pug, Benny, the only
two souls who know the real me and still love me anyway.*

Contents

Part I: The 5 AM Miracle

Introduction 2

Chapter 1: The Miracle of 5 AM 4

Remarkable Benefits of a 5 AM Miracle 6

Find Your Own 5 AM 7

Are You Ready to Dominate Your Day Before Breakfast? 8

The Four Commitments. 9

How to Read This Book 10

A Quick Note about Innovation and Expectations 10

Quick Review: Dominating Your Day Before Breakfast 13

Chapter 1 Action Plan. 13

Chapter 2: In Pursuit of Greatness 14

Comfort: The Enemy of Greatness. 15

10 Exceptional Benefits of Waking Up Early 19

Quick Review: Why Getting Up Early Is So Awesome 27

Chapter 2 Action Plan. 28

Chapter 3: Bouncing Out of Bed
with Enthusiasm 29

Seven Steps to Finally Becoming a Morning Person 30

The Quick-and-Dirty Method 35

Frequently Asked Questions 36

I'm Up, Now What? 39

Quick Review: Night Owl to Early Riser 41

Chapter 3 Action Plan. 41

Part II: The 5 AM Blueprint

Chapter 4: Laying the Foundation **44**

Your Road Map for Success 44

Highest and Best Self 46

Seven Steps for Extraordinary Productivity 47

Step 1: Define Your Life's Grandest Goals 51

Quick Review: The 5 AM Blueprint and Grandest Goals 54

Chapter 4 Action Plan 55

Chapter 5: Forget Annual Goal Setting **58**

Why Long-Term Planning Doesn't Work 59

What Matters Most Right Now 61

Step 2: The Quarter System 62

Quick Review: Your Quarter System 73

Chapter 5 Action Plan 73

Chapter 6: Powerful Lifelong Habits **76**

Habits and the Quarter System 77

Step 3: Anchor and Complementary Habits 78

Connecting the Big Picture with Your Daily Actions 84

Quick Review: Anchor and Complementary Habits 86

Chapter 6 Action Plan 86

Chapter 7: Design Your Ideal Routines **91**

Step 4: Your Ideal Routines 92

The Four Types of Morning Routines 98

Design Your Ideal Morning Routine 100

Quick Review: Design Your Ideal Morning Routine 106

Chapter 7 Action Plan 106

Chapter 8: Rockin' Productivity **109**

Step 5: Productivity Strategies 110

Bringing It All Together 121

Quick Review: The Productivity Strategies 123

Chapter 8 Action Plan. 124

Chapter 9: Tracking Bold Progress 127

Step 6: Tracking Bold Progress. 128

Daily Review 129

Weekly Review 131

Monthly Review 135

Quarterly Review 137

Annual Review. 138

Quick Review: Tracking Bold Progress 141

Chapter 9 Action Plan. 141

Chapter 10: The 5 AM Professional 144

Step 7: Advanced Strategies 145

Quick Review: Advanced Strategies. 154

Chapter 10 Action Plan 154

Part III: The 5 AM Action Plan

Chapter 11: The 5 AM Action Plan. 157

30-Day Plan to Implement Everything. 158

The Summary of Everything: The 5 AM Miracle in Three Steps .166

Quick Review: 30-Day Action Plan. 167

Chapter 11 Action Plan 167

Chapter 12: Time for Bold Action 169

The 5 AM Toolbox. 171

Ambitious Actions List 173

References 174

Acknowledgments 177

About the Author 181

PART I:
THE 5 AM MIRACLE

Introduction

Waking Up Early to Run: A Double Kick in the Pants

. . . and the heavens parted and God said, "Let there be a miracle at 5:00 a.m., let all the people bounce out of bed with enthusiasm, let them dominate their day, and let no snooze button stand in their way."

—A Productivity Junkie's Bible

A few years ago, I was in training for a marathon. I was working a full-time job as a career advisor, building a side business as a productivity coach and podcaster, and finding it increasingly difficult to make time for my daily run. In fact, I was getting so sloppy with my schedule that the only exercise I made time for was the long run on Saturday morning.

As any marathon coach will tell you, the long run is the most important of them all. However, as with most great habits, *consistency is more important than sporadic action*. That meant that I would be better off running a few miles a day, five to six days a week, than impulsively throwing my marathon hopes and dreams into one long and brutal effort.

I needed a new plan. If I was going to be running nearly every weekday and carving out consistent time for my most important goal, I had only a few viable options: run before, during, or after work.

Running during my workday was highly unlikely with only a 30-minute lunch break. If you know me, you know I really like to eat—and eat a lot—and eat often. Skipping lunch was off the table.

The other reality for me, like most people with a day job, was the sheer challenge of navigating a midday workout (lack of access to a gym or shower, transporting workout clothes, scheduling running between meetings, getting my boss to agree to a longer lunch break, etc.). Though technically these were all just excuses, they were also real obstacles that needed real solutions.

Running after work appeared to be my best candidate, but something always seemed to get in the way. I continually planned after-work trips to a local park or the gym, hoping to force myself to stick to a schedule by changing my environment. It did not seem to matter how I finagled my evening routine; consistently working out after a long day at the office proved to be as challenging as running the marathon itself!

Since I was now out of options, I turned to my worst-case scenario: waking up earlier to work out before work. I know, it sounds painful.

At the time I never would have identified myself as a morning person and had the awful habit of waking up at the last possible minute, hitting my snooze button at least twice, and refusing to smile until I had a hot cup of coffee in hand.

Waking up early to run seemed like a double kick in the pants. Who would ever volunteer to do either of those things, let alone both at the same time?

However, as I would soon discover, *waking up early to tackle my grandest goals would be the greatest personal and professional decision I had made in years, and possibly, ever.*

CHAPTER 1

The Miracle of 5 AM

What It Means to Dominate Your Day Before Breakfast

> **Mir·a·cle:** *noun: a surprising and welcome event that is not explicable by natural or scientific laws and is considered to be divine; a highly improbable or extraordinary event, development, or accomplishment.*

Welcome to *The 5 AM Miracle.* I am Jeff Sanders and this is *the* book dedicated to dominating your day before breakfast.

Just like my podcast, also called *The 5 AM Miracle,* this book's goal is to help you bounce out of bed with enthusiasm, create powerful lifelong habits, and tackle your grandest goals with extraordinary energy.

Throughout this book, I will be discussing early mornings and diving much deeper into topics like healthy habits, personal development, and rockin' productivity.

I started my podcast due to one key anchor habit that has revolutionized the way I live: *intentionally waking up early.* This one habit has become the backbone of everything I do.

Over the years, I have given many explanations as to what the 5:00 a.m. miracle is and how it could be defined. From my experiences, there are so many wonderful things about waking up early that it took quite a bit of soul searching to pin this one down.

For the sake of this book and for clarity, the 5:00 a.m. miracle can be defined as *the extraordinary act of dominating your day before breakfast, intentionally bouncing out of bed bright and early in order to make significant progress on your grandest goals.*

In my experience, 5:00 a.m. is a fantastic time of day, and throughout this book, I will strongly emphasize 5:00 a.m. as the ideal time to get up every morning.

However, the act of waking up at that time is not impressive on its own. After all, 5:00 a.m. is arbitrary. However, what 5:00 a.m. stands for is much more impressive, and ultimately, miraculous.

1. 5:00 a.m. is a block of time each morning when life is calm, serene, and peaceful. In the early-morning hours, there are few distractions, the birds are just beginning to sing, and life moves at a slower pace. For some, this is the only time of day they have to themselves.

2. 5:00 a.m. is a symbol for taking control. Realizing your life and your time are in your hands is incredibly empowering and presents abundant opportunity. When you use your minutes wisely, you reach a pinnacle of achievement and fulfillment that few ever do.

3. 5:00 a.m. can become your most precious asset.
When you guard your time and prioritize your tasks; when you optimize your body and develop your mind; when you live on purpose and pursue your grandest goals; you reap the limitless benefits of *the miracle of 5:00 a.m.: a grand life lived with intention, pursued with ambition, and rewarded with transformation.*

REMARKABLE BENEFITS OF A 5 AM MIRACLE

For those who experience their own 5:00 a.m. miracle, there are no accidents. Their life is planned on paper, on purpose, every day, without exception. This also means that the benefits they experience are planned. The amazing results are anticipated and realized.

Though I cannot guarantee your results, I and countless others who wake up early on purpose have experienced truly amazing benefits. You, too, can realize amazing benefits by following the plan outlined in this book.

Depending on what you choose to do with your precious morning hours, you could experience these benefits and more:

1. Dramatic increase in sustainable energy.

2. High-quality sleep and consistent sleep patterns.

3. Weight loss and improved health.

4. Consistent increase in daily productivity.

5. Ability to ward off distractions, especially those that plague all of us late in the day.

6. Improved mood and a positive outlook on your day.

7. Better physical fitness, strength, and endurance.

8. Ability to make phenomenal progress on the goals that matter most to you.

9. Improved mental clarity and creativity, especially in the early-morning hours.

10. Ability to monitor and maintain healthy and productive habits for the long term.

FIND YOUR OWN 5 AM

Before we dive in too deep, let me clarify this point: Though I will certainly make every attempt I can to convince you that 5:00 a.m. is the best time ever to bounce out of bed, *you don't have to wake up at 5:00 a.m.*

All right, take a deep breath and smile!

No part of this book or the plans in it require you to wake up at 5:00 a.m., 6:00 a.m., or any other time before, during, or right after sunrise.

You get to pick your own 5:00 a.m. miracle, which may happen at 7:00 a.m., 8:30 a.m., or as some college students may enjoy, 12:30 p.m. Whatever works for you works for you.

The goal of this book is not to persuade you to set your alarm clock to 5:00 a.m., but rather to open the abundance of opportunity that presents itself when you live each day on purpose. Your daily miracle can happen at any time you choose.

During the process of writing this book, I traveled to New Orleans for a wedding. One morning my friends snuck into my hotel room and took a picture of me sleeping with the alarm clock showing 9:46 a.m., just to prove that I really didn't wake up at 5:00 a.m. every morning.

They find the picture hysterical, but it shouldn't surprise anyone that I don't wake up every single morning at sunrise like a robot. If I stay up late, I sleep in. If I need extra rest, I take it. If 5:00 a.m. is not the best time to get out of bed, then it is not the best time.

The goal is to be intentional—nothing more, nothing less.

Getting all of the quality sleep you need and optimizing the hours you are awake is the name of the game.

ARE YOU READY TO DOMINATE YOUR DAY BEFORE BREAKFAST?

I had a great conversation with a successful personal development coach a while back. He enjoyed my blog and podcast, but he had a concern about my favorite phrase.

In a very straightforward manner he told me that my tagline, "Dominate Your Day Before Breakfast," intimidated him and it was likely scaring away people who could benefit from my message.

Honestly, I was a little surprised. I was going for more of a *super-inspirational-wanna-kick-butt-before-your-day-starts* kind of tagline.

At this point, I am hoping that the idea of domination doesn't frighten you, but rather pumps you up and prepares you for the adventure that lies ahead.

When I picture dominating my day, I can see myself working hard, moving effortlessly from one important task to another, and smiling as I realize how much amazing work I'm getting done.

The truly remarkable thing, even today, is that this scenario happens all the time. When I follow The 5 AM Blueprint (the grand, goal-achieving system that I will break down in Chapter 4), my highly productive morning rituals flow smoothly into highly productive daily workflows and I feel on the top of the world.

In fact, I wrote much of this book during many of my all-star morning routines. I would bounce out of bed at 5:00 a.m., tackle my top early-morning priorities, and then be at a coffee shop, the library, or in my home office writing by 6:00 a.m.

The best part is that after my morning work sessions, I am usually able to take it easy for the rest of the day. This is possible because, at its core, dominating your day before breakfast is all about up-front sacrifice for delayed benefits. In other words, if you work hard (and smart) for a few hours each morning on the tasks that matter most, you can free up time, create mental space, and reduce stress from the rest of your day.

You literally can dominate your entire day within a few hours and then reap the benefits of freely choosing how the rest of your day will go.

With that in mind, it doesn't take much to make domination the norm. In fact, all it takes is a solid plan, a reason to wake up before the rest of society, and a goal that means the world to you.

With those few things in place *you easily have the ability to make your morning routine the most powerful force in your life.* You have the opportunity to use those few precious hours in such a productive way that your life's grandest goals are no longer bucket list fantasies. Instead, those dreams become quarterly objectives (page 62), and making impressive daily progress on those life-altering goals becomes second nature.

That's what I want for you, and I know it's possible.

THE FOUR COMMITMENTS

There are four commitments that I would like you to make as you read this book. These commitments lay the foundation for achieving your own 5:00 a.m. miracle.

1. I will have an intentional and written plan for my day, every day.

2. I will consistently implement healthy habits for optimal energy and enthusiasm.

3. I will choose short-term objectives that help me achieve my life's grandest goals.

4. I will track my progress, make necessary adjustments, and hold myself accountable.

I know, it sounds like a lot. And yes, the fourth commitment is really three in one. However, as you will see in the coming chapters, these commitments will transform into habits. It will become progressively easier to guarantee that these concepts become your reality.

Success in the long run is determined by consistent and well-chosen daily activities. When you make these four commitments you are choosing to optimize today, which will undoubtedly translate into success tomorrow.

HOW TO READ THIS BOOK

I am a voracious reader and I love nothing more than highlighting a book to death. I designed this book to be read just like that. I want you to metaphorically tear this book to pieces as you read it. Pull out your favorite highlighter, pen, or digital scribe and get to it!

Ideally, you will create and update an ambitious actions list as you read the book so you don't forget all of your amazing ideas. I have gone ahead and provided space for that list at the end of the book (page 173), but feel free to take notes in whatever form works best for you.

Also, be sure to take advantage of the action steps at the end of every chapter.

A QUICK NOTE ABOUT INNOVATION AND EXPECTATIONS

I wrote this book, first and foremost, to be actionable and effective, not necessarily shockingly innovative. There are many people who read books expecting to be dazzled with brilliant, mind-blowing concepts handed down on stone tablets. The lessons, strategies, and ideas I present in this book are not new in that sense (maybe in the next book?).

What I share is a compilation of strategies that work in real life. These are concepts that have been applied, tested, tweaked, and optimized. If you are looking for a simple, step-by-step system that will help you control the chaos in your life, this book is for you. If you want to be more productive, healthier, and happier, this book is for you. If you want to wake up early and dominate your day before breakfast, then yeah, this book is definitely what you are looking for.

I also realized after writing the book that it's possible to read every chapter thinking that I wake up early every morning, make zero mistakes, and optimize every free minute like a superhero. Sorry, I'm actually just a normal guy who really likes checklists. Yes, I certainly love to wake up early and get things done. However, I'm not perfect (just ask my wife) and I don't want you to ever believe that perfection is the goal.

Being productive is an endless journey that requires you to wake up each morning and decide again to make today count. Long-term success with *The 5 AM Miracle* is a daily decision, a recommitment to your grandest goals, and an opportunity to begin again each and every time the sun rises.

The cool part is that whatever mistakes, problems, or blunders you have experienced any time in the past don't have to follow you through tomorrow morning. When the rooster crows again at 5:00 a.m. you can literally choose a whole new life path. You've gotta love that!

As you will soon see, I love to summarize big ideas into short checklists. Here is a summary of everything in this book broken down into three simple steps. If you reach a panic point, or you feel a bit overwhelmed, pause and refer back to these three steps.

1. Plan: Map out each day intentionally before it begins.

2. Execute: Make tangible progress through focused blocks of time on your grandest goals.

3. Review: Every week, fully review what you did and what you will do next.

Plan, execute, and review. That's it.

I am already excited to hear your 5:00 a.m. success story!

KILL THE SNOOZE BUTTON
Pitfalls, Mistakes, and Problems to Avoid

Go ahead and sleep in.

In each chapter, I include a *Kill the Snooze Button* section where I share common pitfalls, mistakes, and problems to avoid. These will be actionable tips that will help keep you on track while dodging the bullets that I and others have already taken for you.

To begin, let me recommend my most important piece of advice: Don't wake up at 5:00 a.m. tomorrow!

Don't do it.

I know you want to already. I know it's tempting, but we're not there yet.

In fact, if you are not already on an early-morning schedule, waking up at 5:00 a.m. tomorrow will likely make you hate me and you'll never finish reading the book.

Let's keep both of us happy. Feel free to sleep in tomorrow and get plenty of beauty rest—you're going to need it . . . (can you hear the ominous music playing in the background?).

Okay, it's not that dramatic. But seriously, I will be outlining a very specific, step-by-step plan to show you how to make the transition to becoming an early riser without all the pain you may be anticipating.

I will also outline a plan for the masochist who likes to jump in with both feet and is ready for a serious adjustment.

Either way, tomorrow is your free day. Take advantage of it.

QUICK REVIEW: DOMINATING YOUR DAY BEFORE BREAKFAST

1. The 5 AM Miracle is defined as *the extraordinary act of dominating your day before breakfast, intentionally bouncing out of bed bright and early in order to make significant progress on your grandest goals.*

2. Waking up early has many extraordinary benefits, from being more productive to achieving serenity before anyone else is even awake.

3. To achieve your own 5:00 a.m. miracle, you don't have to wake up at 5:00 a.m.! You can choose your own miraculous time to wake up and dominate your day.

CHAPTER 1 ACTION PLAN

1. Write out the four commitments and post them somewhere you can see them every day:

   - I will have an intentional and written plan for my day, every day.

   - I will consistently implement healthy habits for optimal energy and enthusiasm.

   - I will choose short-term objectives that help me achieve my life's grandest goals.

   - I will track my progress, make necessary adjustments, and hold myself accountable.

2. Grab your highlighter and pen, and dive in!

CHAPTER 2
In Pursuit of Greatness

A Willingness to Do What Works

I'd like mornings better if they started later.

—Garfield

Like many night owl college students, there was a time in my life when I was only awake at 5:00 a.m. because I was still up partying from the night before.

Even as I left school and began working full-time, I still only woke up early if I felt there were no other viable options. I had no love of early mornings or embracing the sunrise. In fact, I would plan my mornings to be as short as humanly possible.

If I had to leave the house for work by 7:00 am, I was awake no earlier than 6:30 a.m. In that 30 minutes I would rush around like the house was on fire, shoving food in my face as I got dressed and styling my hair as I ran out the door.

From where I stand today, it was madness—*sheer madness*.

How did I let myself act like that for so long? How did I miss the opportunity available to me to wake up with intention, with a plan, and with any reason other than survival?

Where I was then is where many people stand today. Their days begin with madness. For them, waking up in a self-inflicted chaos is just another typical morning.

At the other end of the spectrum, there are those who wake up with no plan and no energy. Their mornings consist of piddling around, checking Facebook, and simply wasting hour after hour. They accomplish nothing and arrive at work with little or no ambition to do anything all day.

I know these kinds of people exist because I have been both of them myself at one point or another. It can be so easy to fall into the trap of waking up again and again without a solid sense of purpose, meaning, or direction.

It's disheartening to witness so much potential being thrown away in myself and others, especially when I know that this problem can be solved with only a few simple strategies. Whether a morning routine is a battleground of insanity or nothing more than a few wasted hours, it's not the way mornings were meant to be.

You can do better—much better.

COMFORT: THE ENEMY OF GREATNESS

Whenever I imagine my ideal life, I tend to use the same few words to describe what I want to see: ambition, success, prosperity, and greatness.

Maybe it's the hundreds of personal development books that I have read over the years that have brainwashed me, or maybe there is something there, something deeper.

For years I have been in active pursuit of closing the gap on my potential, seeking to achieve greatness. As a personal development fanatic, I have found that greatness, like success, is a noble goal and worthy of pursuit.

Over the years, it has become clear that simple, daily habits (like waking up early or going for a run) are the backbone to the greatness that I seek. The problem is that on any given day, I am not necessarily in hot pursuit of greatness. Instead, I am looking for the next most comfortable place to rest.

In spite of my success, I routinely find myself going out of my way to avoid hard work, postpone challenges, and eliminate anything that might make me feel uncomfortable. Comfort is addicting. It's easy to achieve and it's everywhere.

Everything being sold, pitched, and dangled at us is another tool, gadget, or gizmo designed to make our lives easier.

Is that what you want?

Do you really want your life to be easier and more comfortable? Or, instead, do you want your life to be more meaningful and your existence to exemplify greatness?

For my own use, I have defined greatness as *the active pursuit of my potential.* Greatness is not a finite position or end goal. It is a process, an ongoing battle, and a daily fight.

You achieve greatness by becoming the highest and best version of yourself every single day. This is not about the perception others have of you, but about how you decide to live your life each morning as the sun rises and to continue that pursuit all day long.

Earl Nightingale, known as the father of the modern personal development movement, defined success as "the progressive realization of a worthy ideal." In other words, if you actively and consistently work toward inspiring and challenging goals that push you toward your own potential, you are successful, and in turn, living a life of greatness.

On one episode of my podcast, I borrowed a brilliant idea from Darren Hardy, publisher of *SUCCESS* magazine, and presented an argument that *focus* is the most important skill in the 21st century. I also described how distractions are the greatest enemy to focus.

In our world today, comfort may be the ultimate distraction and the defining enemy of greatness. Nothing will cause you to give up faster, let your guard down sooner, or simply lose focus with greater ease than comfort.

Your brain's natural desire is comfort, tradition, and sameness, which is why habits can become so powerful and automatic.

It takes real work to overcome your natural tendencies and avoid comfort, which ultimately holds you back from growth. Comfort does not assist in your growth; instead, it actively works against you.

Eating fatty foods, drinking alcohol, borrowing money, staying up late, watching TV, and avoiding awkward social interactions are all examples of our natural desire to take the easy road instead of the right one.

You have a choice. The alternative to these examples is less sexy, and that's what makes them so unappealing in the short term and so powerful over the course of our lives.

- Instead of eating fatty foods, you could order a salad.

- Instead of drinking alcohol, you could opt for water.

- Instead of borrowing money, you could save up the cash for later.

- Instead of staying up late, you could go to bed early.

- Instead of watching TV, you could read a fascinating book.

- Instead of walking away from a conversation, you could engage in an intriguing dialogue.

It's true, the alternatives to our natural tendencies are less sexy. They are uncomfortable and require us to work just a little harder. However, these simple, daily choices are the same ones that make a powerful difference when applied consistently over time, and they are the same ones that ultimately lead to greatness.

You have a choice. You can seize these growth opportunities or fall victim to the easy comfort that follows you around like a cute puppy.

To achieve greatness and fight its opposing force of comfort, you will have to lean into the pain and, at least to a small degree, lean into masochism.

Masochism is "the enjoyment of what appears to be painful or tiresome." When you embrace masochism you acknowledge and even appreciate the growing pains.

Over time you can overcome the tendency to lean toward comfort by training your "masochism muscles." You can literally train yourself to enjoy the growth process as you strengthen your resolve and transform into a higher and better version of yourself.

I'm not arguing that you will actually become the kind of person who enjoys pain, but that you can strengthen your ability and willingness to push through when times get tough instead of backing off or giving up altogether.

You will get more done when you have stronger muscles and can repel the distraction of comfort. You can also be more productive and successful if you train yourself to build the energy, systems, and muscles to do the hard work every day.

The process of training your masochism muscles is a series of habits. It is the act of doing small things every day in many areas of life, which eventually lead to significant growth in the long run.

Over the course of this book and throughout The 5 AM Blueprint (page 47), I will challenge you to push yourself. There will be plenty of opportunities for you to form new habits, take on new projects, and adopt new philosophies, all of which can strengthen your masochism muscles.

In the context of becoming an early riser, the connection is obvious: Waking up early is going to hurt. I'm not going to make this sound easy because it's likely that you will want to give up and quit on me.

Don't do that.

What hurts today may not hurt at all in the future because your muscles will have grown stronger, more powerful, and more resilient.

This is not an impossible project, and yet, it's not something you will want to attempt passively either. Significant change requires significant investment. The good news is that you can achieve that change slowly over time, and through the form of this book and my podcast, I'll be with you the whole way.

10 EXCEPTIONAL BENEFITS OF WAKING UP EARLY

Waking up early is awesome and there are dozens of amazing benefits that make a 5:00 a.m. wake-up call worth it. If you're still on the fence about it, here are the top 10 benefits that should easily push you over the edge:

1. MORE TIME TO PLAN YOUR DAY AND EXECUTE IT EFFECTIVELY

Of all the reasons to wake up early, this may be the most practical on Day 1. When you wake up even just 15 minutes earlier than normal and you use that time for planning your day, you are already entering domination mode.

While the late risers are thrashing out of bed at the last minute, scrambling to find their toothbrushes and briefcases (does anyone use those anymore?), you have created a written plan for exactly how your day will go. You know ahead of time what to cut and what to keep. You know when your appointments are and what resources you will need. You know the optimal order of events for the day because you have optimized your schedule and updated your task list.

Creating an intentional, prioritized, and written plan for your day is everything. Planning how you will use your time is the number one strategy for achieving your own 5 a.m. miracle. It is the most important element in this book and it is the key difference-maker between success and failure.

If you haven't already done so, highlight that last paragraph. *That's gold, baby!*

2. PERFECT FOR QUIET TIME

The early morning hours are likely the only time you will have to yourself all day long. For many people, this is it. The time between 5:00 a.m. and whenever the rest of the family wakes up is the golden hour. This is your chance to soak up a few precious moments for those activities that easily get lost in the shuffle later in the day.

Whether you choose to read, meditate, pray, practice yoga, or any other quiet activity, make the most of it. Light a candle, play soft music in the background, or just sit in silence.

For years I refused to meditate because I thought I was too much of a busybody to be good at it. What I have found over the last few years is that quiet time is essential for collecting my thoughts, lowering my stress levels, and maintaining my own peace of mind. Even if you, like me, identify as a productivity junkie, type A personality, or ambitious high achiever, don't neglect the benefits of slowing the pace of your life—even if it's only for a few minutes.

3. HIGHER-QUALITY SLEEP AND MORE CONSISTENT SLEEP PATTERNS

When you embrace a consistent wake-up call, you will have no choice but to embrace a consistent bedtime in order to get the sleep you need. One great side effect of transitioning to this life-style is that your sleep is likely to improve.

There are many factors that affect sleep quality, but consistency is one of the most important. Waking up early forced me to prioritize going to bed, which forced me to prioritize ending my work day earlier, which forced me to be more intentional and efficient all day long. You see the pattern here? Setting even just one firm boundary in your day can have a ripple effect on every other choice you make.

Getting better sleep is all about consistency and preparation. Knowing you have to be in bed by a certain time will also cause you to prepare for bed, which means your mind and body will be ready to rest.

4. MORE ENERGY AND OPTIMISM

I know a lot of people (*cough*, me, *cough*) who don't look too pretty in the morning. On top of my hair being a mess, weird goop being stuck to my eyelashes, and some of the worst bad breath you can imagine, I also don't naturally bounce out of bed with a goofy grin on my face.

That used to be the case every day, but now it's a rare occurrence. A typical wake-up call involves me literally bouncing out of bed with enthusiasm as I begin my morning routine. This isn't genetics at work. *I was not born this way.* This is all about habits, systems, and choices.

This is a concept that bears repeating again and again: *The best morning routines prioritize energy* because it is the foundation for productivity. Energy is a natural by-product of amazing health and it's awesome!

This may be the type A, espresso-loving, perky man in me, but why would you want to feel exhausted when you could feel pumped up? Why would you want to lie on the couch when you could be out for a run? Why would you intentionally hold yourself back when you know that the power behind your journey forward is nothing more than sustainable energy?

We will discuss the specifics in Chapter 7, but just note that if you want to fill your mornings with more joy and optimism, you can do it. You can choose to bounce out of bed smiling. It is certainly possible and worth the effort.

5. BETTER FOCUS

Assuming that when you wake up at sunrise you truly are the only person awake in your house, you have a shining opportunity in front of you. One of the greatest benefits of waking up early is the unmistakable lack of noise and interruptions. There is nothing standing between you and your goal. There are no distractions unless you create them.

There are many people who begin their day with television. They wake up and immediately turn on a morning talk show, the news, cartoons, or a rerun of a late-night comedy special they missed.

If your goal is focus, concentration, and execution, distractions like these have to go. The phenomenal benefit of focus is it's always available, unless you choose to opt out. Focus is all about the elimination of everything except the one thing that matters most. Embrace the simplicity of a focused morning routine and you will experience those benefits over and over again.

6. BETTER BRAIN: IMPROVED MENTAL CLARITY AND CREATIVITY

Have you ever tried to do something really important late at night? How did that work for you? If you're anything like me, you have to fight to think. Thinking clearly is more difficult and often painful when your brain is tired.

I know from years of trial and error that my best mental acuity is available to me during the first half of the day, not the last. This is true across the board. In *The Willpower Instinct,* Kelly McGonigal describes how willpower is a finite resource that replenishes itself when we sleep. As the day progresses, our reserves of discipline and our desire to work slowly diminish. We find ourselves less capable of performing simple tasks without exerting intense effort.

If you want to take advantage of the natural cycles your brain is already going through, then jump at the chance to do your best work early in the day. It doesn't necessarily have to be right when you wake up—just don't wait until happy hour to start writing your next novel.

7. SEXIER AND HEALTHIER BODY

My best morning routines are either focused on a major project or my health. When I'm not using 5:00 a.m. to read, write, or finish an urgent project, you can find me drinking green smoothies, running trails, and hanging upside down from my gravity boots.

The morning hours are ideal for taking care of yourself. Most people either squeeze in a few minutes here or there for a quick trip to the gym, or they just never make the time for self-care. Of all the things you could do at 5:00 a.m., eating a healthy breakfast and exercising should be at the top of the list.

Waking up early is not a magic weight-loss solution, but the trend is that the kind of people who wake up early are also the kind of people who exercise. People who exercise are the kind of people who eat healthier. People who eat healthier tend to lose weight, and people who lose weight tend to have more self-confidence and feel sexier.

That's how it has worked for me and countless others, and that's how it could work for you too.

8. CONSISTENT INCREASE IN DAILY PRODUCTIVITY

One of the most fascinating side effects of waking up earlier is the residual effect of increased productivity all day long. When you start your day with intention, it's likely you will finish it that way too.

There are days when I sleep in (obscene, I know!). On those days I am usually never as productive as the days when I wake up earlier. It's like clockwork. When I wake up with a plan, I also work my day with a plan. When I wake up and wing it, I get the results you would expect—subpar.

If you want to keep yourself chugging along all day, executing tasks like a five-star general, then it's best to begin your day the way you want to end it. Start with intention and productivity, and finish with intention and productivity.

9. MORE LIKELY TO ACCOMPLISH YOUR GRANDEST GOALS

Being productive means that you are getting things done, but simply doing more is not your primary goal with *The 5 AM Miracle*. What happens when you wake up earlier is that you open the doors of opportunity. You can literally do anything. Time has been freed up that previously never existed, which leaves you with a choice.

You can either optimize that time or squander it. You can make the most of it or let it pass you by. The trick is to predetermine how you will spend your time. The people who wind up getting more done with their own 5 a.m. miracle are also those who wake up with a solid plan to make progress on their life's grandest goals.

You have the ability to make phenomenal progress on the goals that matter most to you when you block off time for your highest aspirations. You have time for running a marathon, writing a book, building a business, studying for grad school, or any other worthy pursuit.

Even just one hour a day, five days a week can be enough to make progress on something that is valuable to you and your mission. Take advantage of that time and guard it like the crown jewels.

10. YOU WILL JOIN AN EXCLUSIVE CLUB OF HIGH ACHIEVERS

What do Howard Schultz (CEO of Starbucks), Richard Branson (founder of the Virgin Group), Anna Wintour (Editor-in-Chief at *Vogue*), and Tim Cook (CEO of Apple) all have in common? Outside of their amazing success in business, these four power players are also early risers. Richard Branson and Anna Wintour wake up at 5:45 a.m., while Howard Schultz and Tim Cook rise at 4:30 a.m.

Don't forget famous notables such as Benjamin Franklin, Thomas Jefferson, Margaret Thatcher, Barack Obama, George W. Bush, Frank Lloyd Wright, and Charles Darwin.

There is a clear connection between intentionality and success, between early risers and high achievers, between waking up with a plan and changing the world. If you want to begin your journey to high achievement, waking up early should be the first task on your list tomorrow morning.

KILL THE SNOOZE BUTTON
Pitfalls, Mistakes, and Problems to Avoid

Give yourself the appropriate title.

Before I was a marathon runner, I wasn't. Before I was a podcaster, I wasn't. Before I was an author, husband, college graduate, or any other descriptor—I wasn't.

You don't become someone new until you live it. You can't call yourself an athlete, high achiever, or early riser unless you actually walk the walk (or run the run).

When I first considered making running part of my lifestyle, I had one major obstacle in my way: I didn't think of myself as a runner. In fact, not only would I never have used that term to describe myself, I was scared to do so.

"Runners" were elite athletes. They were slim, fast, and super skilled at something I couldn't imagine doing myself (or, at least, doing well).

In the summer of 2006, after returning home from a study abroad program in Prague, I was in the worst shape of my life. I quickly decided to make running the central focus of my new fitness regimen. I ran a little bit every day in the beginning, usually no more than five minutes at a time.

By the end of that summer, I was running five miles a day. Was I a runner? I thought so.

Was I a runner when I was only running five minutes a day? Not according to me.

It wasn't until I was running five miles a day that I allowed myself the privilege of referring to myself as a runner.

I don't know why I set that boundary, but I did. It was arbitrary and it drew a line in the sand. It was my indication of real progress.

My story of becoming a runner is the same story you share when you become someone new. One day, you would never refer to yourself as an early riser, and the next day, it is part of your vocabulary. Nothing significant changes on the outside, but something dramatic shifts within.

Start small and let yourself off the hook. That's all it takes to make the critical shift of significant change. Begin by believing in what it means to embody your new title and don't hold yourself back from embracing it quickly.

I waited far too long to refer to myself as a runner. Five minutes a day is the same as five miles—both indicate action and both exemplify what it means to walk the walk.

Even serious night owls can one day refer to themselves as early risers.

QUICK REVIEW: WHY GETTING UP EARLY IS SO AWESOME

1. You will have the precious time you need to effectively plan your day.

2. Early mornings are ideal for meditation, prayer, yoga, or just a little quiet time.

3. Your sleep is likely to improve dramatically with consistent bedtimes and wake-up calls.

4. You will almost certainly have more energy and a more positive attitude.

5. It's easier to focus on your biggest goals.

6. With improved mental clarity, your creative juices will flow even faster.

7. Early risers tend to exercise more, eat healthier, and have a sexier body. What's not to like?

8. Getting more done is nearly a guarantee when you wake up prepared to dominate your day.

9. With a consistent 5 a.m. miracle in place, you are more likely to achieve your life's grandest goals.

10. Many high achievers wake up early and you are about to join them.

CHAPTER 2 ACTION PLAN

1. What does a typical morning look like in your world? Busy and stressful? Slow and peaceful? Productive and exciting?

_____

_____

_____

_____

2. Is your life too comfortable? What are your comfort tendencies, those habits and rituals that steer you away from greatness?

_____

_____

_____

_____

3. What benefits appeal to you the most from an early-morning lifestyle? Why get up early at all? What are you hoping to achieve at 5:00 a.m.?

_____

_____

_____

_____

CHAPTER 3
Bouncing Out of Bed with Enthusiasm

How to Finally Become a Morning Person

I stay up late every night and realize it's a bad idea every morning.

—Unknown

The most common question I receive is from night owls. They hear me preach the benefits of waking up early and are still left with the nagging question, "As a night owl, can I really make the switch and wake up early?"

Simple answer: Only if you want to.

The time you wake up each day is not a genetic trait. It's not part of your DNA and it's not predetermination or fate holding your head against the pillow every morning.

Consistently waking up early is a skill, which is great news. That means you can actually improve your abilities over time, and see real progress.

In short, you can follow a simple set of steps and make the transition happen, no matter how late you currently go to bed or how early you want to wake up.

Becoming a morning person is a real thing and it's really possible—even for you night owls.

SEVEN STEPS TO FINALLY BECOMING A MORNING PERSON

Now that I've convinced you that waking up early is not only worth your time, but is also a killer strategy that can lead to wild, long-term success, here are the seven steps that will take you from a late-night junkie into an early-morning fanatic.

1. DRINK THE KOOL-AID AND EMBRACE YOUR INNER FLANDERS

Ned Flanders is my favorite character from the television show, *The Simpsons*. Mr. Flanders is the dork of all dorks with his big glasses, annoying voice, and obscenely perky personality.

He is friendly, organized, and lives according to his "three Cs": clean living, chewing thoroughly, and a daily dose of vitamin church. To truly become a morning person, it's best to think like a morning person. It's time to embrace your inner Flanders and do what he would do.

If you decide to skip this step and deny that even a small part of you really likes Mr. Flanders, you may end up waking up early for the wrong reasons. In the beginning you will be fine, but over time your progress will fade and you will likely give up. Without a passionate *why* in place—your deep-seated and compelling reasons for a 5:00 a.m. wake-up call—you will find any excuse to sleep in and negate the benefits that we just discussed.

It's all about what's at stake. If your life's grandest goals matter to you, then bouncing out of bed with enthusiasm should matter even more.

ACTION: Let's say you are not a fan of Mr. Flanders, but there is a successful early riser that you would love to model your life after. Use that person and drink their Kool-Aid. Become the next Thomas Jefferson or Margaret Thatcher by studying their life, habits, and successes. Follow in the footsteps of the most successful person in your industry or the person who you believe embodies an awesome future version of you.

2. TRAIN LIKE THE TORTOISE

The funny thing about making any significant life change is that it's easy to do once. You can run a marathon without training. You can borrow money without a plan to pay it back. You can pull an all-nighter tonight and finish a big project.

The problem is that all of these short-term choices have swift and painful repercussions.

Running a marathon without training might garner you a finisher's medal, but it will hurt worse than any pain I can imagine. You won't walk for days and you'll likely never run again.

Borrowing money without a payment plan leads to credit card debt, sleeping on your parents' couch, and bankruptcy. Sounds good now, hurts big time later.

Not sleeping tonight, even if it results in massive progress on an important goal, will destroy your calendar for the next few days as you recover. I've experienced my fair share of all-nighters and I always regretted not planning more effectively ahead of time.

None of these are long-term solutions. All of them are impulsive and nearly useless when aggregated over time. It's better to break large projects into tiny pieces and plan to work for the long haul.

Becoming a successful early riser is not a spontaneous or whimsical decision—it's a way of life and a way of thinking.

If you want to succeed this week, next year, or in 50 years, you'll need a solid plan to get you there.

ACTION: Get out your calendar and begin the shuffle. Knowing that your sleep patterns are going to change, plan ahead now for how that will look in the long run. What goals would you like to work on early in the morning? What tasks have you scheduled late at night that need adjusting?

3. SEND YOURSELF TO CAFFEINE REHAB

I love coffee. Specifically, I love a double espresso every morning. When you make the switch to an early-morning routine, you may have to temporarily adjust your daily caffeine levels.

I consider myself a bit of a caffeine addict, so I know how you feel if this sounds like an impossible task. The good news is that you don't have to give up coffee to wake up earlier. However, if you want to make the transition easier, you may find it helpful to minimize how much you drink so that you can fall asleep earlier each night.

The earlier you fall asleep, the earlier you can wake up. The logic here is sound, but the emotional toll of less caffeine is a bit tragic. Sorry!

ACTION: Cut back on the quantity of caffeine you drink every day and set a daily boundary for caffeine consumption. For example, I only drink caffeine in the morning and don't allow myself to have any in the afternoon so that I can fall asleep faster.

4. RESCHEDULE LATE-NIGHT ACTIVITIES

When I was in college I would routinely swing by Taco Bell for a late-night snack. I would shovel down burritos, enchiladas, and 44-ounce fountain drinks. It's hard for me to stomach the idea of eating anything like that now, but I'm not the same person I was then.

Look at your own late-night habits and determine when they can happen earlier in the day, if at all. Watching too much TV? Cut it. Surfing Facebook until 1:00 a.m.? Not anymore. Staying out late with friends on a week night? Sorry, it'll have to wait until Friday.

In order to make this transition as smooth as possible, simply reschedule your favorite late-night habits. You do not have to cut out television and social media forever, just refrain from gorging on large helpings after your bedtime.

ACTION: Make a list of your current late-night activities. What do you consistently do that you know you could reschedule, minimize, or stop altogether?

5. BUILD A BOUNDARY AND GET TO BED

The most effective way to wake up early is to go to bed early. The best way to ensure you stick to your bedtime is to destroy the obstacles between your busy, working self and your tired, lying-in-bed-with-your-eyes-closed self.

I created a late-night boundary just for this reason. 8:00 p.m. is my stop time. At exactly 8:00 p.m., I will turn off whatever I am working on. This includes my computer, phone, TV, iPad, and any other technology.

At this point, I would have either finished my tasks for the day or rescheduled them for another day. I would have also created my task list for tomorrow and responded to all of my emails (I'll discuss Inbox Zero in Chapter 8). I then take a shower and grab a book to read before heading off to bed.

This evening routine is a written process. It is planned in advance, tweaked over time, and optimized so that I can get to bed on time every night without fail. Are there exceptions? Of course, but the odds of success increase dramatically with a well-planned and routinely updated structure in place.

ACTION: On paper, plan your ideal evening routine. Write out what you will do and when you will do it. If necessary, create a boundary for stopping all work for the day. Share this plan with anyone who lives with you or who likes to send you late-night tasks from the office. (Hint: Tell your boss about your new sleep schedule so he or she doesn't keep you up until midnight.)

For a more detailed description and instructions on creating your evening routine, refer to Chapter 7 (page 91).

6. TURN BACK THE CLOCK JUST A LITTLE

This is where the shift begins. Set tomorrow's alarm clock just 15 minutes earlier than usual and update tonight's bedtime to 15 minutes earlier as well. This is a small baby step toward the long-term goal of waking up at your ideal time.

If your current bedtime is around 11:00 p.m. and you would like to transition to be asleep by 9:30 p.m., plan that 90-minute shift in 15-minute increments. It's best to not even notice the transition, so don't get up earlier until the new time feels normal.

Also, don't worry about how long this process might take you. Just change the times when it feels right. Depending on your schedule and your body's response to the shift, you could be up at your ideal time tomorrow, next week, or many weeks from now.

ACTION: Plan your first 15-minute time shift. Set a definite bedtime and a corresponding alarm clock time that aligns to how much sleep you need for optimal rest.

7. WAKE UP AND DO SOMETHING POSITIVE

As you transition, plan a new healthy and productive activity you will do during those 15 minutes. If all you do is wake up earlier to continue with the same routine you have always done, nothing will have changed except the times you were asleep. The goal here is increased productivity and tangible results.

You could spend those extra 15 minutes doing any habit that makes sense to you, but I would recommend you initially focus on something you have been missing out on. If you love yoga but can't seem to make the time, then practice yoga for 15 minutes tomorrow. By doing something you love, you will end up appreciating that time way more than you might imagine.

To begin, make a list of morning habits you would like to adopt, or habits you can reschedule from later in the day to first thing. Some of the best morning habits are ones that help you wake up with energy and a positive frame of mind. I recommend choosing something calm and peaceful, like meditation, prayer, or reading a positive book.

Alternatively, you could move your body right away through Pilates, a brisk walk or run, and a few rapid-fire push-ups. I have found that incorporating a short but intense workout in my morning routine is a surefire way to transition to an earlier wake-up time. If you want to make your transition easier, more effective, and faster, be sure to schedule a workout in your morning routine.

ACTION: Plan the healthy habit you will do with your new 15 minutes of freed-up time. You don't have to choose just one. You could cycle through a list of habits you would like to do less often than once a day, like "Meditation Mondays" or "Trail Run Tuesdays."

THE QUICK-AND-DIRTY METHOD

If you tend to describe yourself as a masochist and the idea of a gradual transition to an early morning lifestyle seems painfully slow to you, I have a solution.

Repeat all seven steps that I just described with one major exception: Modify step 6 so that you wake up at your ideal time tomorrow morning.

With this simple change you will feel like every international traveler: jet lagged, wickedly tired, and happy to have finally made it.

The first few days are going to hurt, but it won't last long. I recommend scheduling those first few days with tasks and projects that don't require a lot of brain power (and maybe even take a few days off work). Catch up on household chores, mindless tasks, and anything you can do by yourself. Consider it a favor to your family and coworkers that you are working out your fatigue and bitterness without them.

Don't forget to adjust your bedtime according to your sleep needs and new wake-up time. You may also find that it's easier than ever to fall asleep early now that you are desperate for a little shut-eye.

FREQUENTLY ASKED QUESTIONS

Q: How long will this transition take?

A: It's totally up to you. With the quick-and-dirty method, you can be up at 5:00 a.m. tomorrow, or you can slowly transition over the course of weeks or months. Depending on your schedule and how determined you are to make an early morning part of your lifestyle, this can happen whenever it works best for you.

Q: Do I have to wake up early seven days a week? What about the weekends?

A: Here's the beauty of *The 5 AM Miracle* at work. No, you certainly don't have to wake up early every single morning. Being intentional with your time is the name of the game, which means you can wake up whenever you want.

However, if you really want to become a thriving morning person, your sleep schedule should be as consistent as possible. If you normally wake up at 5:00 a.m. on weekdays, then waking up at 11:00 a.m. on Saturday would throw off your internal clock in a big, bad way. I'm not recommending you throw out your social calendar and become a hermit on Friday nights, but if productivity matters to you, there will be sacrifices.

The good news is that you can be flexible and still maintain positive habits over time.

Q: What's the minimum number of hours you think that I should sleep? Won't I be more productive if I sleep less to maximize my day?

A: Though I'm not a sleep doctor, I can say with certainty that everyone is a little different when it comes to how much rest they need to recover fully each day. My wife, Tessa, needs a considerable amount of sleep, ranging between 9 and 11 hours per night. I only need about 7 to 8 to feel well rested and ready for the day.

You likely already know your body and know how much sleep you need to wake up refreshed. The goal is to get that ideal amount of sleep as often, and as consistently, as possible.

Your daily productivity will become a horrible disaster if you sacrifice sleep for too long. Accomplishing your life's grandest goals is a long-term game. Sometimes a short-term sacrifice is worth it, but sleep is a magical thing. Do your best to maintain a healthy rhythm of rest and your body will thank you.

Q: If I go to sleep late, should I wake up early even if I didn't sleep the minimum number of hours?

A: I love this question because it's indicative of the desire to stay committed to your goals. The problem with waking up early in this scenario is that it backfires quickly.

You will likely never hear me tell someone to wake up at sunrise after going to bed well after midnight. It just doesn't add up.

What ends up happening is massive sleep deprivation, regret, and a serious lack of productivity. When you lose sleep you also lose the ability to think clearly, make intelligent decisions, and stay primed to do your best work.

When you find yourself in this unfortunate circumstance, sleep in. Get the rest you need and return to your normal early mornings over the course of the next few days.

Q: What if I wake up late? Have I missed my chance to be productive? How should I approach the rest of my day?

A: Waking up late is going to happen. It happens to everyone, including me. The goal is not to avoid waking up late, but rather to optimize the hours you are awake.

Though you won't miss your chance to be productive if you wake up late, you will likely miss a few key habits you have established for yourself early in the day. What works best is to let it go. Be okay with missing your morning workout today and move on.

There will likely be other chances later in the day to make up anything you missed that morning, and you can always get back on track tomorrow.

Never let any one individual day dictate your overall goal trajectory. Stay focused on the big picture and getting back to your routine as soon as you can.

Q: What about the rest of my family? What if I'm married, or have kids, roommates, dogs, and three pet gorillas at home? How do I get up early in my busy home?

A: There are two answers to this question. First, if you have pet gorillas at home, Wow! I need to meet you. Second, living with other people who are on different schedules than we are is not an excuse to sleep in or slack off on our own goals.

We all have battles to fight, obstacles to overcome, and bizarre circumstances to navigate. In the few years after college, I moved across the country to work over 70 hours a week between two jobs while running marathons and starting a side business. *I know what it's like to be busy.*

I have also thrived in various seasons of my life when I lived with my family, various roommates, and even 30 fraternity brothers in a party house that never slept. *I know what it's like to navigate my goals and schedule around other people.*

Sitting back and passively letting something stand between you and your goals is a choice. At the same time, it's natural and healthy to acknowledge where you are in life. There are seasons, trends, and temporary situations that may prevent you from having the ideal life you want.

At the same time, to quote Albert Einstein, "In the middle of difficulty lies opportunity." There will always be solutions buried in the chaos. There will always be amazing ways to make progress that you never saw before but that now seem to shine brightly because you changed your perspective.

Whenever I feel stuck or burdened by my circumstances, I look for the new perspective. I ask myself, "What am I missing? If I absolutely had to, how could I solve this problem?"

If you ask the question, the answer always appears. It may not be what you want to hear, but it's there.

I'M UP, NOW WHAT?

Assuming you have followed the seven steps and transitioned to an early-morning routine (or are about to get started), what should you be doing with your precious, new early morning hours?

In Chapter 7 (page 91) I will outline a few simple steps to structure your ideal morning routine from top to bottom. We will look at examples of great routines, discuss how to align your morning routine with bigger life goals, and put your routine through the gauntlet to guarantee it is the best it can be.

Before we get to the specifics of your 5 a.m. miracle, in the next few chapters we are going to explore the heart and soul of your new productive life with The 5 AM Blueprint.

Waking up early is the face of this book, but an early-morning routine is merely one piece of a bigger system, one that has the potential to transform your entire life into a goal-achieving machine.

KILL THE SNOOZE BUTTON
Pitfalls, Mistakes, and Problems to Avoid

All right, here it is—no more snoozing.

There's a good reason why I named these segments "Kill the Snooze Button." Snooze buttons are the greatest metaphor for beginning your day backward.

The norm for most people is starting off each morning with the decision to procrastinate by smacking their alarm clock and delaying the decision to bounce out of bed and dominate their day.

Snoozing inadvertently becomes a reactive choice, which leads to further reactivity. When you begin the day reacting to your environment instead of proactively shaping it, you find yourself on the defensive. Everything is a fire to be put out, a problem to be solved immediately, and in a very short timespan, you can find yourself overwhelmed, stressed out, and behind schedule.

Where did the time go?

Why did I forget to meditate, run, or read my favorite book?

What happened this morning?

The snooze button creates this scenario and furthers the belief that mornings are awful, when in fact it is the way we approach our day that needs a massive transformation.

My recommendation is simple: Stop snoozing altogether. Wake up and get up.

No more snoozing.

No more sleeping in past your predetermined wake-up call.

No more delaying the beauty of the morning and the opportunity to accomplish your grandest goals.

This is the beginning.

QUICK REVIEW: NIGHT OWL TO EARLY RISER

1. Find your own Ned Flanders, follow in his or her footsteps, and embrace your inner morning person.

2. Like a tortoise, you are in this for the long run. Prepare now for the journey to come.

3. I love caffeine too, but it's time for a mini break. Cut back on the coffee for just a bit.

4. Trips for burritos at midnight are out. Identify all of your late-night habits that need adjusting.

5. Set a firm boundary and make your evenings count. Waking up early depends on going to bed early.

6. Begin the shift. Set your alarm clock for your new wake-up call. Slowly transition or jump in feet first—your call.

7. There's great power in a great workout. To make this shift easier, plan now to exercise in your new early morning.

CHAPTER 3 ACTION PLAN

1. Create an effective set of evening rituals (including going to bed earlier than usual) and then do those rituals tonight.

_____

_____

_____

_____

2. Set tomorrow morning's alarm 15 minutes earlier than usual.

Your current time:

_____

Your new time:

_____

3. Decide on *one* new ritual you are going to do in that 15 minutes.
Your new ritual:

_____

_____

PART II:
THE 5 AM BLUEPRINT

CHAPTER 4
Laying the Foundation

Preparing for an Epic Adventure

From early childhood I had always dreamed of becoming an explorer. Somehow I had acquired the impression that an explorer was someone who lived in the jungle with natives and lots of wild animals, and I couldn't imagine anything better than that! Unlike other little boys, most of whom changed their minds about what they wanted to be several times as they grew older, I never wavered from this ambition.

—John Goddard, adventurer, explorer,
author, and ambitious goal-achiever.

YOUR ROAD MAP FOR SUCCESS

Unlike John Goddard, I was definitely one of those little boys who changed his mind about his future many times. I even wrote an entire book about it, called *Graduated and Clueless*. My life story is one of experimentation, not focus. I love variety more than making a firm decision and I am quick to admit that I don't really know what I'm doing.

What I am sure about is that when I do make decisions, I learn from the experience. I pay attention to things that pique my interest and I follow my passions down every dark alley and dirt road. Like John Goddard, my life is a grand adventure, but it is based more on curiosity than confidence. I may not always know what I want, but I know I'm willing to try just about anything to figure it out.

Two months after I graduated from college, I moved over 1,000 miles from my home in Missouri to the thriving metropolis of Boston, Massachusetts. I had no job, no money, and no plan. What I did have was the willingness to do whatever it took to make Boston my new home. Growing up in the Midwest, I had always dreamed of moving to a big city. When an opportunity popped up (by way of my then-girlfriend-now-wife getting into grad school), I jumped at the chance to redefine my life as a Bostonian and soon-to-be Red Sox fan.

Within a few days of moving into my absurdly expensive apartment, I landed a job in door-to-door sales. Let's not sugarcoat this—I searched through Craigslist to find a job that literally anyone could get. I didn't have a car and my commute took 90 minutes each way on Boston's subway. I promptly quit my job after nine painful weeks, having only sold products to a handful of customers.

My one saving grace in this wild experience was my boss. He was obsessed with John Maxwell, the well-known public speaker and author of over 70 books. My boss gave me one of John Maxwell's books, *Your Road Map for Success*. He asked me to read the book in a few days and report back with any lessons I had learned.

This was my turning point. Having spent the first 23 years of my life dreading having to read anything, this was the first book that fully captured my attention and flipped my perspective on what it meant to live a life of success, achievement, and real purpose.

My greatest discovery was the world of personal development. John opened my eyes to the reality that I could choose my future, forge my own path, and create the life I had always wanted. That may sound like exaggerated hippie talk, but the transformation that took place inside my mind was nothing short of revolutionary.

HIGHEST AND BEST SELF

My relentless pursuit of personal growth is one that is aimed at the highest point: becoming my best self. There is no other scenario that makes sense to me. Why would I shortchange my own potential when I could genuinely reach higher and higher?

Over the years I have put myself through many experiments in an attempt to reach higher. I have radically changed my diet, fitness, faith, and lifestyle. I have run ultramarathons, toyed with juice fasting, and read hundreds of books on topics ranging from starting a side business to mastering fancy yoga poses.

What has surprised me most, however, is the fact that my greatest epiphanies and successes are not based on brilliant innovations of the caliber that could solve world hunger.

What was true years ago, and what is still true today, is that my greatest accomplishments are born out of the most fundamental processes.

In the introduction of this book, I told a story about training for a marathon by waking up early to run before work. I concluded the story by saying that *"waking up early to tackle my grandest goals would be the greatest personal and professional decision I had made in years, and possibly, ever."*

Waking up early is not a unique or brilliant innovation and it certainly won't cure cancer or end homelessness. But the break-through I experienced revealed that bouncing out of bed at 5:00 a.m. could be the ticket to unleashing your greatest self.

Like a tiny hinge that swings open a big door, waking up early can provide the leverage for doing just about anything you can imagine, including making tangible progress on the goals that will define your future and push you closer to your highest and best self faster than anything.

SEVEN STEPS FOR EXTRAORDINARY PRODUCTIVITY

After years of waking up early to pursue my life's biggest goals, I formalized my best ideas, strategies, and processes into a step-by-step system I call The 5 AM Blueprint. It consists of seven steps for extraordinary productivity and lifelong goal achievement.

This is a solution to your daily chaos: a little calm in the storm, and potentially, the foundation upon which you can rest your productive future. That's a bold statement, so let's dive into the specifics so you can see exactly how this works in the real world.

Here are the seven steps in the Blueprint. The next several chapters will expand upon each of these steps and provide specific actions you can take to bring these concepts to life.

The 5 AM Blueprint

1. **Define Your Life's Grandest Goals**

   The pyramid, though overused as an illustration, is actually a great way to think of the Blueprint. The foundation rests on your life's grandest goals. We will break down how to identify those later in this chapter.

2. **Create Your Quarter System**

   The second step is to create a Quarter System, in which your goals are broken down into quarterly checkpoints (page 62). That will proactively transform your dreams and fantasies into concrete, actionable projects.

3. **Identify Key Anchor Habits and Their Complementary Habits**

   The third step is to identify your key anchor habits, which will naturally flow into productive complementary habits. All of these habits form the structure of your day and lead to increased productivity, energy, clarity, and many other great benefits.

4. **Create Your Ideal Week, Ideal Morning Routine, and Ideal Evening Routine**

   The fourth step is to create your ideal routines in the form of an ideal week, ideal morning routine, and ideal evening routine. This is where the 5:00 a.m. miracle kicks in and where you will specifically and intentionally optimize your most precious hours of the day.

5. **Implement the Most Effective Productivity Strategies**

   These will be incorporated in various forms throughout your day and will be strategically connected to your grandest goals.

6. **Track Your Progress with the Most Effective Tools**

   Throughout the goal-achievement process, this is where

you will measure, monitor, and manage your ideas, tasks, and projects.

7. Go Pro by Implementing Advanced Strategies
The seventh and final step is to optimize the entire system with advanced strategies. Once you have mastered the previous steps you will be able to integrate strategies that will take your success to the level of a 5:00 a.m. pro.

IS THE BLUEPRINT RIGHT FOR YOU?

The 5 AM Blueprint is more than just a series of strategies or a pretty pyramid. At its core, the Blueprint is a worldview. It is a lens through which you see how your smallest actions and choices can add up to big results.

My podcast listeners, blog readers, and coaching clients are examples of ambitious people who see the world as I see it—a wide-open opportunity. The Blueprint is a system for people who are hungry to seize the opportunities they know are right in front of them.

If you are hungry for success, achievement, service, or even just for eliminating chaos from your life, the Blueprint will provide a framework to take advantage of the opportunities that are all around you every day.

WHAT "POINT A" AND "POINT B" REALLY LOOK LIKE

To provide a context for the Blueprint, let's walk through a not-so-extreme example of a fictional character I'll call Busy Betty.

Right now, Busy Betty is at "Point A." She has a full-time job, kids at home, personal goals, fitness goals, and business aspirations, and her life is a train wreck. She feels overwhelmed, she can't keep up, she's always behind schedule, and she drops the ball frequently because she has ineffective systems in place—or none at all.

She wants more from her life but feels like she's drowning in responsibilities, commitments, and her own ideas. There is always too much to do and never enough time. There are always more emails to respond to, more events to attend, and more projects to work on than she will ever have the capacity to even just begin, let alone complete.

In short, Busy Betty is in desperate need of a miracle.

Now let's take a look at Busy Betty at "Point B," after she has fully implemented The 5 AM Blueprint and been using the system for a few months. At this point, Busy Betty is organized, efficient, and clear about her daily objectives. She has connected the dots between her short-term schedule and her long-term aspirations, not to mention she has a thorough and written plan in place.

She has review systems and solid accountability incorporated efficiently into her lifestyle. She utilizes effective productivity strategies to improve her daily output and she has good healthy personal habits in place to maintain her energy and fitness. She wakes up with a plan each morning and knows how to optimize her schedule so that she can spend as much time as possible on her top priorities.

Now, at Point B, Busy Betty's life is not perfect, but the contrast from Point A is startling. She has taken the reins of her life and regained control.

Busy Betty is now Much Better Betty.

Your life may not be quite as chaotic as Busy Betty's, but that simply means you will be able to adopt these strategies and get real results even faster than she did.

On that note, let's jump in to the first step of The 5 AM Blueprint and get this party started!

STEP 1: DEFINE YOUR LIFE'S GRANDEST GOALS

An epic adventure begins when you specifically define where you are going. Like most people, you may have found yourself wandering from one goal to another without any sense of connectedness. There is no visible through-line, story arc, or clear objective.

The best stories (and the best lives) have clear end results. There are specific missions to embark on and those missions are tied to a bigger picture. No one goal stands alone because it is part of an epic journey.

When I refer to "grandest goals," I am referring to goals that move your soul. They are clear and ambitious dreams that will shortly become tangible projects.

The grandest goals are not items on a bucket list because bucket list goals usually end up as end-of-life regrets. They fall into the category of "I wish I would have . . ." or "Why didn't I …," and those phrases are not part of this process.

PERSONAL OPTIMIZATION PLAN

Before putting together your grandest goals list, you may find it helpful to clearly articulate what your life would look like when it's firing on all cylinders.

Begin by creating your Personal Optimization Plan (POP), or set of scenarios, environments, and/or circumstances when your life is working like a well-oiled machine.

- What does the highest and best version of yourself look like?

- What are you doing?

- Who are you with?

- What are you passionate about and working hard on?

- What are you doing when everything is working well?

When you know what you life looks like when it's flowing beautifully, it's much easier to imagine which characteristics are true about your life. You will be able to articulate your income, location, friends, achievements, and passions.

CREATE YOUR GRANDEST GOALS LIST

Now is the time to make your list. Go to the whiteboard, get out a notebook, fire up the computer, or start using your favorite brainstorming tools.

The initial list that you create should be crazy long. Don't hold yourself back or filter as you work. Let every thought end up as a viable idea. You can always remove the idea later, but filtering in your head is an example of limiting, which only leads to you denying yourself the right to dream.

Don't do that. Feel free to think like a kid and fly to the moon. Be the fireman, princess, or astronaut you always knew you would be.

Here are a few questions to help you create your goals list and clearly identify the grandest goals in your personal and professional life.

1. What have you always wanted to do but never made time for?

2. What would you be amazingly proud of after it is completed?

3. What have other successful people you admire accomplished that you would like to emulate?

4. What does your POP look like?

5. What scares *and* excites you when you think about it?

6. What have you tried to do in the past but failed to finish?

7. If you had no obstacles with time, money, or energy, what would you attempt?

8. If you had a magic genie at your disposal who could grant you one wish, what would you ask for?

9. What brings you incredible joy and would only be amplified if you took it to the next level?

10. What is the one thing you are thinking of right now that you know needs to be on this list?

KILL THE SNOOZE BUTTON
Pitfalls, Mistakes, and Problems to Avoid

Don't stop believing.

It's all too common to encourage children to dream big and then to turn around and chastise adults who never grew up. Dreaming is not reserved for 6-year-olds who want to be astronauts or teenagers who want to solve world hunger.

Grand goals are for all of us, and when we stop believing in our own ability to dream, we stop believing in the ability of others to do the same.

What amazes me is that most goals generally require a similar amount of effort. Why, then, do we assume that pursuing our fantasies is a pipe dream? Why do we assume that shooting for the stars is reserved for someone else?

In the process of establishing your grandest goals, don't stop believing in your own abilities. Go ahead and assume that each of the grand goals you're already thinking of are too small because they probably are.

You can do more and you can do better.

One of my personal grand goals is to run the 100-mile mountain ultramarathon in Leadville, Colorado. It's one of the most brutal courses in the world and easily ranks as one of the most challenging personal goals I can imagine.

Ken Chlouber, cofounder of the Leadville race, is famous for saying, "You're better than you think you are and you can do more than you think you can." That spirit embodies the heart of any grand goal and especially the goal-setting process.

Don't stop short of dreaming big simply because you believed you were never capable to begin with.

QUICK REVIEW: THE 5 AM BLUEPRINT AND GRANDEST GOALS

1. Pursuing the highest and best version of yourself is the ultimate goal and waking up early accelerates that process.

2. The 5 AM Blueprint is a step-by-step system for dramatically increasing your productivity and helping you achieve your life's grandest goals.

3. If you are hungry for success, achievement, and service, the Blueprint is right for you.

4. Identifying your grandest goals is as simple as thinking like a kid again, letting yourself fly to the moon and back.

CHAPTER 4 ACTION PLAN

1. How do you develop yourself on an ongoing basis? How often do you read great non-fiction books, magazines, or articles, or attend conferences, mastermind groups, or other personal experience endeavors where you intentionally develop skills, character, and other worthy traits?

_____

_____

_____

_____

_____

2. Create your POP, a set of scenarios, environments, and/or circumstances when your life is working like a well-oiled machine. What does the highest and best version of yourself look like?

_____

_____

_____

_____

What are you doing?

_____

_____

_____

_____

Who are you with?

_____

_____

_____

_____

What are you passionate about and working hard on every day?

_____

_____

_____

_____

What are you doing when everything is working well?

_____

_____

_____

_____

3. Make a list of your life's grandest goals (both personal and professional) and the current grand goals you are working on today. Your grandest personal goals:

_____

_____

_____

_____

Your grandest professional goals:

_____

_____

_____

_____

Grand goals I'm working on right now:

_____

_____

_____

_____

CHAPTER 5
Forget Annual Goal Setting

How to Achieve Your Grandest Goals Now

We mistakenly believe that there is a lot of time left in the year, and we act accordingly. We lack a sense of urgency, not realizing that every week is important, every day is important, every moment is important. Ultimately, effective execution happens daily and weekly!

—Brian P. Moran, author of *The 12 Week Year*

In 1955 Cyril Northcote Parkinson, a British political analyst and historian, observed that "work expands to fill the time available for its completion." This adage is known as Parkinson's Law and the lessons from this simple principle can have a profound effect on how you approach accomplishing your tasks in a timely manner.

From a productivity standpoint, this could mean you either have very little time and are forced to rush or you have more than enough time, which leads to rampant inefficiencies.

It's a rare day when any of us schedules the exact amount of time we need to complete a task. Most people are notoriously terrible at predicting how long a project will take, and when given more time than necessary, they take it.

But why?

It's human nature. We're lazy. We want the easy answer and we want to believe we will be more productive tomorrow than we feel like being today. We believe that since we have "plenty of time" to work on a project, we can postpone the work to an arbitrary future date. The problem is that today is yesterday's tomorrow. We are living out the fantasies of our past right now. Yesterday you probably thought you would have more time today than you do. Today you most likely believe that you will have more time tomorrow than you will. That's the nature of the beast.

The reality is that time is finite. It's running out quickly, and you only have the present moment to pounce on the goals you care so much about. Instead of planning life far in advance and believing there is a lot of time left to finish your important projects, you need to flip your perspective and get to work today.

WHY LONG-TERM PLANNING DOESN'T WORK

The most common approach to setting goals is sitting down once a year to write out New Year's resolutions. What this means is that on January 1, you begin to work on projects that may not be due until December 31.

How motivating is a due date that's a year away? How much is at stake if you don't make progress today, tomorrow, next week, or even next month?

On top of the lack of urgency, you also have no idea how your year will actually unfold. You have little or no control over what projects will pop up, what ideas you will have, or what opportunities will capture your attention, energy, time, and money.

Tim Cook, the CEO of Apple, was asked about his experience with creating a 25-year plan during graduate school. During the interview that took place 25 years after he graduated with his MBA, the interviewer asked Tim, "How did that [your 25-year plan] work out for you?"

This is how Tim responded:

"[My 25-year plan] was reasonably accurate for all of 18 to 24 months after it was written. Not a single thing on it was accurate after that. Not a single thing. Zero. The lesson there, at least for me, was that the journey was not predictable at all."

Tim Cook is arguably one of the most powerful men in the world and he could not have predicted that he would be where he is today. What does that say for long-term planning? Not much.

One of the best books on productivity I have ever read is *Getting Things Done* by David Allen. David's philosophy about how to be as productive as possible is a phenomenal lesson in perspective.

From a practical perspective, I suggest going from the bottom up, instead of top down. I have coached people from both directions, and in terms of lasting value, I can honestly say that getting someone in control of the details of his or her current physical world, and then evaluating the focus from there, has never missed.

What this means is that in order to eventually solve your 25-year problems, you need to first solve your 25-minute problems. In the book, David goes on to explain that when he helps a client take control of their daily tasks, they feel incredibly more confident, positive, and hopeful about their long-term future.

If you wanted to embrace this methodology as a way to plan your next couple of decades, start by first planning the next few hours, and then the next few days, and then maybe even the next few weeks.

Over time, as you improve your ability to plan your short-term schedule, it gets easier to plan the big picture. But, as we have seen with Tim Cook, there is certainly a point of diminishing returns. In other words, you may be able to effectively plan the next 30 days, but planning the next 30 years will be considerably more difficult and, in many ways, it would actually just be a waste of time. Many people fear their long-term future but they do little in the present moment to change anything about their circumstances.

Ask yourself, "If I continue down the path that I am on right now, where will I end up in 5, 10, or 20 years? Is that somewhere I want to be?"

Gaining clarity like that can make a huge difference in how you tackle your individual tasks on a day-to-day basis.

WHAT MATTERS MOST RIGHT NOW

The reason that New Year's resolutions and 25-year plans don't work is that when you think too far ahead to a future you can't control, you set expectations that don't align with your ideal self.

You shortchange your potential when you plan years in advance by dreaming of goals that are either extraordinarily too far out of reach, which paralyzes you in fear, or even worse, goals that are so mediocre and boring that you have no enthusiasm to get moving.

When you plan our life too far in advance you often envision an idealistic future devoid of problems and obstacles while ignoring the real opportunities that are right here in the present moment.

It's like shining a tiny flashlight into a deep, dark pit. You can see very little in front of you and are left guessing about everything beyond your reach. The farther out that you try to plan your life, the more you are forced to just make stuff up to fill in the gaps. On top of that, you then commit to too many projects in the present that don't align with your goals for the future, causing you to be real busy without making any real progress.

Attempting to achieve your life's grandest goals by planning everything out years in advance is just simply not the answer.

Let's take another look at the grandest goals list you created in Step 1 of The 5 AM Blueprint (page 51).

Those goals on your list are potential projects. They are ideas, fantasies, and future possibilities. You are now going to transform those concepts into reality with an effective goal-achievement system that will clarify what matters most right now and leave everything else for another day.

In effect, this is a system that facilitates real progress, here and now, on your most important goals because it eliminates the inefficiencies of long-term planning.

I introduce the Quarter System.

STEP 2: THE QUARTER SYSTEM

What would happen if you only had one big goal right now? How would that change your life? Would you be less stressed? More focused?

What about 10 goals? Or 100 goals? Is that workload manageable today, or even over the course of an entire year?

What I have found to be true over and over again is that simplicity always wins. There is no scenario where adding more to my plate makes me feel better, unless I literally have nothing going on.

More likely than not, you and I both don't lead lives that need *more* things to do. Instead, what we need are drastic cuts to stay afloat, focus, and eventually, make tangible progress on our grandest goals.

An extremely simplified list of grand goals combined with a significantly shorter timeframe is your ticket out of the chaos. It is the healthier and more productive alternative to setting annual goals or making multi-year (or multi-decade) plans.

The Quarter System is the second step of The 5 AM Blueprint and it is as simple as it sounds. Instead of setting annual goals, you will set quarterly goals.

Now, you might be asking, "But, Jeff, I already have annual goals and quarterly goals. How is this any different than what I am doing now?"

First, if you already have a solid written plan for the year and your goals are broken down into quarterly checkpoints, *and* you are staying on track with your plan, then you are light-years ahead of the game and should probably be coauthoring this book with me.

Second, when I refer to quarterly goals, I am referring to them in the same way that Brian Moran does in his book, *The 12 Week Year*. In the book, Brian describes a year as lasting only 12 weeks, which is equivalent to three months, 90 days, or one quarter. (I will refer to this system in quarters, but feel free to use any length of time that helps you focus best. That's the goal, after all.)

In practical terms this means that you will think of a quarter as a year—nothing will be scheduled after that time period unless it has to be, and you will work as hard during the current quarter as you normally would at the end of a 12-month year.

What most people tend to do is create a New Year's resolution in January and then work like crazy on it in November and December because they procrastinated for over 10 months. The goal with a year that lasts only 12 weeks instead of 12 months is that it puts that kind of pressure on you right away. You are forced to prioritize, get laser-focused, and get to work immediately because the clock is ticking.

TYPICAL QUARTER SYSTEM TIMEFRAMES

- January 1 to March 31

- April 1 to June 30

- July 1 to September 30

- October 1 to December 31

I am tempted to suggest that you choose a different length of time for your year, like 60 days, 120 days, or even just shoot for living day-to-day with no thought beyond the next 24 hours. But there is magic in a Quarter System.

The business world operates in quarters, which makes it easy for you to align your deadlines with those of your peers. You also have enough time over three months to tackle seriously challenging projects, like starting your own business, writing a book, or training for a marathon.

A lot can happen in 90 days, and yet, it's only a small window of time that needs to be handled carefully so you don't squander too much of it.

MY EXPERIENCE WITH THE QUARTER SYSTEM

My personal experience with the Quarter System has been nothing short of revolutionary. I don't want to exaggerate the benefits here, but simplifying my already highly productive life to a Quarter System changed everything.

Over the course of a few days, I cut over a dozen projects from my personal goals list and began focusing on just four of them. I completed two of those projects in the next few weeks and then slowly added a few more only as I had time.

The most immediate benefit was my attitude and stress levels. I felt more in control and less nervous about my immediate future. The more tasks, projects, and goals I cut from my task manager, the more free I felt to begin working on the projects that needed my attention most.

This is more of an art than a science and I certainly had to improve my own skills of learning to let go. It's just so easy to get attached to goals, even if you have never made progress on them.

Before I discovered *The 12 Week Year* I had already been using a system that was very similar to it, just without the formal title. I began implementing a Quarter System as my personal goal-achievement program about six months after I launched my podcast. Truth be told, I waited way too long.

The sheer volume of projects I committed to was crazy. In that year alone, outside of launching the podcast, I began my coaching practice, overhauled my diet and fitness routines, ramped up and then quit my short career in real estate sales, and switched my website over to JeffSanders.com (which can be crazy if you, like me, have no experience in web design).

The first step I took when I implemented the Quarter System was to simplify my projects down to the bare essentials. I cut fluffy projects and postponed long-term goals. I focused on my present circumstances and began whittling myself out of the messes I had created.

The secret to any great productivity system is simplicity, and the Quarter System delivered on that promise. I prioritized my ideas, ignored the ones that were not both urgent and important, and then began tackling the next project at the top of my now very short list.

Prior to the Quarter System, I had thought it would be best to simply keep taking on new projects just so I would feel more productive. I'll be the first to admit that setting a goal to feel productive is ridiculous. The only value that feeling productive can bring to the table is motivating you to want to feel that way again. However, the slippery slope is that feeling productive simply leads to low-value tasks landing on your to-do list in place of high-priority tasks that move the needle.

A Quarter System has a funny way of prioritizing your time and eliminating much of the busy work that brings about the good feelings of getting things done. I'm not saying that feeling productive is a bad thing, just make sure it's for the right reasons. At the end of the day, the questions you ask yourself should be related to effectiveness, not emotions.

- Did I make real, tangible progress toward my most important goals?
- Did I stay on track and avoid distractions?
- Did I get the most value out of my day today?
- Could I be more efficient tomorrow?

Checking off a long to-do list is shallow productivity. A focus on quantity instead of quality leads to CHS: Clean House Syndrome. Whenever I want to consciously avoid doing my most important work, I clean my house. Maybe it's the type A in me that wants a clutter-free environment, or maybe it's the lazy man in me that wants to do anything except the work I know I should be doing.

As ironic as it sounds, on a great and productive day, my house is visibly messy. On a lazy day—spotless.

To get the most out of your Quarter System it will be essential for you to harness the skill of focusing on what matters while remaining blind to what doesn't.

HOW TO SET UP YOUR QUARTER SYSTEM

The Quarter System is very simple to set up, implement, and maintain for years to come. Here are the seven steps to get your Quarter System up and running:

1. Choose the Dates for Your Quarters

You can choose any dates you wish, but it's likely going to be easier to stick to the traditional quarters used by most people (January 1, April 1, July 1, and October 1). Depending on the date you are reading this, you can either start now and finish the current quarter you are in or plan to start at the beginning of the next quarter.

2. Clear Your Calendar

Eliminate everything you can from your current calendar to make space for the grandest goals that are most pressing. It's likely that you will need to finish out the current quarter by completing the projects to which you have already committed. For example, if there are six weeks left in the current quarter and you are training for a half marathon and planning a wedding, then finish out those two events and start with a fresh and clear calendar next quarter.

This is an ideal time to cancel plans, eliminate unnecessary tasks, and begin saying no to any new invitations. As hard as it is to let go and say no, it's the only way your calendar will remain open for your grandest goals.

3. Choose Your Top Two or Three Grandest Goals

Based on the list you created in the last chapter, choose only a couple to focus on—possibly even just one goal for now. Without a doubt this was the hardest part of the process when I went through it the first time. Choosing only your top goal(s) among dozens or hundreds of ideas is tough, but this is the dividing line between success and failure.

This is where you will begin to see the magic of creativity appear as you free up space in your head for thinking and space on your calendar for working. If you continue to operate with too many goals you will continue to stretch yourself too thin and see little progress.

You may have a goal or two that will take longer than a quarter to complete. For example, you may be training for a marathon and you know it will likely take 6 to 12 months. In that case, just as you normally would do with a traditional annual goal, break down that goal into milestones and choose an appropriate milestone to reach by the end of the quarter.

4. Create Your Next Actions List by Planning Your Goals in Reverse

Now that you have chosen your quarterly goals, it is time to plan those goals backward from the end of the quarter until now. Simply make a list of every major objective that needs to be completed from the finish back to the start in order to guarantee you complete the goal by the end of the quarter or sooner, if possible.

During this step, be as specific as possible. Not only should your goal be specific, but also each step along the way should be as laser-focused as you can imagine so that there is no ambiguity around what your next step will be.

5. Set Up Your Goals Notebook

You can set up a Quarter System right now with whatever tools you currently use. I am going to recommend and refer to the tools that I use, but feel free to stick with anything that you know is effective for you. I transitioned to a paperless lifestyle years ago and Evernote is one of the core pieces of my system. Evernote is a digital application that manages just about any notes you can imagine. Inside of Evernote you can create "notes," which go inside of "notebooks," which are inside of "stacks."

As an alternative to Evernote you could also use Google Drive, Microsoft OneNote, traditional paper notebooks, or one of many other systems. Regardless of what system you choose, here is an effective way to set up, implement, and manage your Quarter System.

First, create (or find) a notebook and label it with the name of the current quarter (e.g. "2016 Q1 Goals"). Then create a note/page for each grand goal you plan to complete this quarter. The first section in the note will be the "next actions" list you made in the previous step. Below the next actions list is a progress reports section where you will record what progress you made each week.

Run a Marathon

NEXT ACTIONS

1. ☑ ~~Sign up for the race~~

2. ☑ ~~Create my running training plan~~

3. ❑ Meet with my personal trainer to discuss my plan

4. ❑ Buy new running shoes

5. ❑ Train each week

6. ❑ Prepare my supplies for the race day

7. ❑ Run the race on this date _____

PROGRESS REPORTS

Week	Date	Measurement, milestone, or note
1	4/1/2016	Signed up for the race
2	4/8/2016	Created my training plan
3	4/15/2016	
4	4/22/2016	

6. Schedule Your Next Actions on Your Calendar and/or Task Manager

I manage all of my tasks, projects, events, and commitments in a digital task management application named Nozbe. I will go into much more detail about that system in Chapter 8 (page 109). For now, just note that once you have created your next actions list, you will schedule those actions on your calendar and/or in your task management system.

The key here is to take the list of next actions from your goals and make them real by scheduling them. Once a task ends up on a calendar it should be treated like a firm commitment that cannot be broken.

Assuming you truly have cleared your calendar and scheduled each next action at its most opportune time, your odds of success will increase dramatically. This is where you will begin to see the progress I have been talking about. This is where the work begins to feel like fun!

7. Review Your Progress Weekly and Quarterly

I will go into much more detail about how to track all of your tasks, projects, and goals in Chapter 9 (page 127). For now, here is a quick overview of what to review each week.

At the end of each week and quarter, it's best to review the progress you made on your goals and update your progress reports in your notebook. Then, based on what you accomplished and how fast the end of the quarter is approaching, choose your next actions for each goal in the upcoming week. If you have an accountability partner, coach, or friend that you discuss your goals with, this is a great time to review your progress with him or her as well.

On a related note, I also post my weekly goals on my vision board (page 150) in my home office, just so I have a visual reminder of what I am working toward. This has helped keep me on track every week. Having a physical list certainly reinforces the digital system.

RINSE AND REPEAT

At the end of each quarter you will have the chance to fully review your progress, make notes about what went well and what did not, and then start over fresh next quarter.

Ideally, you will have completed the few grand goals you set out to complete and can begin the new quarter with new grand goals that are now the most pressing in your life. This process repeats itself over and over every 90 days and it works wonders.

It was hard for me to imagine how effective this system would be until I tried it. The act of clearing your calendar is rejuvenating in and of itself. When you then add in only the goals that matter and you proactively track your progress toward the completion of those goals, it's nothing short of remarkable. The progress you will make is going to blow your mind. Trust me.

KILL THE SNOOZE BUTTON
Pitfalls, Mistakes, and Problems to Avoid

Don't drown in your own commitments.

It's easy to take credit for your successes but quite the opposite when it comes to your failures. It's never easy to point the finger at yourself when you have made a mistake, missed a deadline, or just never got around to finishing something you started.

What I find most intriguing is that it's nearly impossible to get anyone to admit that they are overly busy because of their own choices. We like to play the victim and believe that being busy is normal, expected, or worse, unavoidable.

The reality, though, is that if you are too busy, it is because you committed to too many things. You made your schedule, said yes to too many projects, and refused to turn down all those enticing invitations to happy hour, holiday barbecues, and dance-till-you-drop weddings.

If you want to turn things around, free up your schedule, and avoid being buried in work, then just say so. Say no to the next invitation or pointless office meeting, no to the next party or social event that keeps you up late, and no to the next anything that doesn't align with the highest and best use of your time.

I'm not recommending that you quit your job, totally avoid your friends and family, and strive to do as little as possible. However, that's the kind of creative space that leads to the breakthroughs you will need to avoid drowning in your own commitments.

Be willing to let go and say no. Clear your calendar and only begin to refill it with the tasks, projects, and goals that are essential to achieving what truly matters most in your life.

QUICK REVIEW: YOUR QUARTER SYSTEM

1. Parkinson's Law tells us that we spend more time than we need to when the time is given.

2. New Year's resolutions and 25-year plans are unpredictable and ineffective, and they never quite work as intended.

3. Implementing a Quarter System can help you focus on your grandest goals, which are those projects that will have the biggest impact on your life now and far into the future.

4. You can set up a Quarter System right now with a notebook, day planner, and Post-it notes, or go digital with Evernote, a calendar in the cloud, and a task manager.

CHAPTER 5 ACTION PLAN

1. Using your list of grandest goals from Chapter 4, choose two or three goals to focus on this quarter (or next quarter if it's fast approaching). These goals are now your new quarterly goals.

1) _____

2) _____

3) _____

2. Clear your calendar and task manger of every task and project that doesn't directly align to your new quarterly goals.

Your calendar will be cleared on _____ (date)

Your task manager will be cleared on _____ (date)

3. Analyze each quarterly goal, breaking it down into tiny baby steps in your preferred note-taking application (Evernote, One-Note, etc.).

Quarterly Goal #1

_____

_____

First few baby steps to get started:

_____

_____

_____

_____

Quarterly Goal #2

_____

_____

First few baby steps to get started:

_____

_____

_____

_____

Quarterly Goal #3

_____

_____

_____

First few baby steps to get started:

_____

_____

_____

_____

CHAPTER 6
Powerful Lifelong Habits

The Energizing Daily Rituals That Transform Body, Mind, and Soul

The chains of habit are too weak to be felt until they are too strong to be broken.

—Samuel Johnson, English author, poet, and journalist

I was an obsessive child. I always had to be first at everything, I refused to let different foods touch on my plate, and I had rigid sleep habits.

On one particularly memorable Friday night when I was just nine years old, my family and I went to a high school football game. This was one of those epic crosstown rival matches there was no way any of us was going to miss.

Late in the second half the score was close, the tension was high, and everyone in the stands was on their feet. I was screaming just as loud as anyone—cheering, booing, and stomping my feet. At one point near the end of the game, my mother looked over at me and saw something rather remarkable: I was asleep standing up.

In the middle of the chaos and having just been wide awake only a few moments before, I had fallen asleep standing on both feet at exactly 9:00 p.m.

At this point in my life, I had the most structured sleep patterns of anyone I knew. Like clockwork, I would fall asleep every night at 9:00 p.m. and bounce out of bed at 6:00 a.m. the next morning. You could literally set your watch to my daily routine.

Those impressive habits didn't stick around during my teen years and I have had to start over from scratch ever since. Yet, among the many differences between my life as a nine-year-old boy and a man in his 30s, there is no doubt that I still have the same ability today that I did back then.

What has changed is that I have had to be very intentional with my habit formation, focusing closely on what it means to create effective, healthy, and productive habits. Most importantly, it is clear that any repeated daily action can become a strong habit that can stick like glue.

HABITS AND THE QUARTER SYSTEM

Your daily actions tell your whole story. Whether good, bad, or ugly, you are where you are today because of your habits, actions you consistently repeat and that are hard to give up. If you truly want to know where you will be many years from now, you only have to look as far as your strongest habits—the actions that have the most impact and that you have repeated more than any other.

Habits are the backbone of your personality, relationships, health, finances, and career. For all intents and purposes, your habits created your life as you know it. Phrased another way, the only thing standing between you and your highest self are better habits.

The key to forming better habits is *conscious consistency*, deliberately choosing effective actions to repeat over and over instead of letting accidental bad habits form. Every day we have a lot more power and control over our lives than we think, but only *if* we think.

As we discussed in the previous chapter, the Quarter System is based on a short vision of the future. However, over time those quarters will add up to a year, two years, five years, and more. The habits that you consistently execute each quarter will determine your success many quarters (and years) from now.

The whole point of the Quarter System is to cause action to happen, and happen faster. When you have chosen goals that are important to you and there is an inherent sense of urgency to get those goals accomplished, it's much easier to bounce out of bed on a daily basis and execute your most vital habits.

After all, if repeated daily actions determine your habits and your habits determine your future, then your daily actions are the most important element between you and the achievement of your grandest goals.

Now, all we need are a few intelligently chosen daily actions to repeat over and over that will lead to securing your strongest, stickiest, healthiest, and most productive habits.

STEP 3: ANCHOR AND COMPLEMENTARY HABITS

In the first step of The 5 AM Blueprint, you established a comprehensive list of your grandest goals, and then, in the second step, you focused on just a vital few goals with your new Quarter System.

In order to reach your grandest goals, you will need more than focus and more than a few marathon work sessions. In the end, daily actions make the biggest difference.

The third step in the Blueprint is the implementation of habits, specifically anchor habits and their resulting complementary habits.

In addition to being handsomely rewarded for your actions, getting habits to stick is as simple as implementing the right reminder (also known as a trigger or cue) that leads directly to the habit itself. The best possible reminder is one that is already in place and that doesn't require you to make any changes at all.

Anchor habits are those habits that are already in place. They are actions you are already doing, and the best part is, they naturally lead to other habits, which I refer to as complementary habits. For example, an anchor habit could be flossing your teeth (assuming you do this regularly), which then naturally leads to the complementary habit of brushing your teeth (because you are already in the right place, at the right time, with the right resources available).

Though anchor habits are typically habits you already have in place, you can also create new anchors, change old anchors, or eliminate anchors that are not working well for you.

There are three core anchor habits that are vital to your success with The 5 AM Blueprint. These are likely anchors that are already in your life in some form. If not, now is your chance to reinvent your day.

The first anchor habit is waking up with a plan. As we discussed previously in the book, how early you wake up is highly subjective. However, the intention behind your wake-up call is not. When you wake up with a plan you then flow easily into the completion of your ideal morning activities, which are your complementary habits.

In other words, one well-chosen activity (the anchor) leads to many other well-chosen activities (complementary habits) that might not have happened unless the anchor was in place.

For example, let's say that you normally wake up at the last minute, rush around the house, and then leave for work without a written plan in place. After implementing the lessons in The 5 AM Blueprint, you wake up earlier and plan your morning efficiently around a few powerful habits. In your past life you never had time for meditation, reading, or exercise, but because of your new anchor habit you now have time for the habits you had been missing.

The second anchor is exercise. Some people work out religiously while others just regret spending money on a gym membership they never use. Though I'm not as consistent as I would like to be, I do prioritize exercise and I recommend it as an essential ingredient in The 5 AM Blueprint. Exercise is a fundamental tool for both health and productivity.

As an anchor habit, exercise lends itself to healthy complementary habits. In my own life I know that when I go out for a morning run I also tend to practice yoga, hang upside down in my gravity boots (which is awesome by the way), eat a healthier breakfast, and shower before work.

Exercise improves your chances of better self-care, eating a better diet, and having better hygiene, among the multitude of other health benefits directly related to fitness.

The third core anchor habit is beginning your workday. That's right, just getting out the door and into the office is an essential ingredient. It seems so obvious, but let's look at why just getting to work is such an effective strategy.

When you go to work, what do you do there? Get to work, I would presume. On the flip side, what do you do when you stay home? Could be anything but work.

When you think of beginning your workday as an anchor habit, you then think about all of the complementary habits that naturally occur: answering emails, attending meetings, finishing your big project, and everything else. When you postpone getting to the office, you also postpone or eliminate all of the essential complementary habits that would have followed.

Like a great story, the key is to think about the inciting incident, the hinge that swings the big door, or any other metaphor where one pivotal action leads to the accomplishment of so many more essential actions. Successfully executing just a few core anchor habits each day has a profound effect on all the other tasks that now become available to complete.

If you have been kicking yourself for neglecting something important, simply implementing the right anchor habit can be the difference between success and failure.

HABITS OF THE HIGH ACHIEVERS

Now that I have covered the three core anchor habits (waking up with a plan, working out, and getting to work), let's discuss some of the healthiest and most productive habits that are widely implemented by high achievers and early risers alike. Though we will specifically discuss productivity strategies in Chapter 8 (page 109), these habits form the foundation for a highly productive day.

Through my podcast I have interviewed dozens of highly successful people, including Dean Karnazes, David Allen, Bob

Proctor, Rich Roll, and more, and asked each about their most effective daily habits. These are the habits that came up again and again through nearly every conversation. High achievers don't waste much time, so when they prioritize a habit it's because that habit brings with it a phenomenal return on investment.

This list is far from comprehensive, but these are the best of the best. When in doubt, go back to the fundamentals and work through this list as often as you can.

1. Bounce Out of Bed Bright and Early

You guessed it, high achievers are early risers and early risers are high achievers. I reiterate this point here because it stands to show just how widespread waking up early is among people who get a lot done. Not every successful person has a 5:00 a.m. wake-up call, but many of them do. It's a clutch habit.

2. Hydrate Like You Live in the Desert

I have been waking up and drinking a liter of water for years, and many productive people do the same. After sleeping for many hours your body is likely to be dehydrated and craving water. A few years ago I implemented the habit of drinking 1 liter (34 ounces) of water before I have my morning espresso. I love my morning caffeine kick, so knowing that I have restricted myself to only getting my reward after drinking the water forced that habit to stick quick.

3. Quiet Time Is Essential

Without a doubt many, if not most, productive high achievers incorporate some form of meditation, prayer, and/or affirmations in their morning routine. Though these three habits are obviously different, they share the similarities of calm, focused thought on something positive and inspirational. That's the goal and it works wonders.

4. Fruit for Breakfast

Every morning I have a 2-liter (68-ounce) green smoothie (fruit smoothie with leafy greens) for breakfast. It's how I have begun my day for the last few years and I can't imagine a better beginning to my day. High achievers focus on quality nutrition early in their morning routine. A healthy breakfast fills your mind, body, and soul with the nutrients you need to thrive.

It would be a disservice to you if I failed to mention my diet as a part of this strategy. In my mid-twenties I went through a radical health transformation, moving from highly processed and cooked animal products to a low-fat, raw vegan diet.

I know that what I eat is not for everyone, but it has been fundamental in my own 5 a.m. miracle. As I have mentioned, a large green smoothie is a staple in my morning routine, and that is because eating large quantities of fresh, ripe, raw, and organic produce is nothing short of life-changing. From increased energy and improved digestion to weight loss and dramatic fitness gains, consistently eating more food direct from Mother Nature is one of the healthiest habits I can imagine.

5. Consume Inspirational and Informative Content

This is unanimous. I can't imagine a successful person who doesn't include some form of personal growth in their day. From audiobooks and podcasts during a morning run to reading books, blogs, and inspirational texts while sipping your morning coffee, consuming quality information is absolutely essential for a productive life. I call my personal growth time my Morning Workshop, and I scour material looking for something actionable for my day—and I always find it.

6. Pump Your Blood

Even if it's for only 10 minutes, morning exercise is a habit that cannot be replaced by anything else. Some high achievers are rather extreme with their fitness, but for most it's highly effective to get the most bang for your buck. Burst training (or HIIT: High Intensity Interval Training) is a great strategy for anyone who does not have a lot of time but wants a great workout. Burst training involves explosive exercises with quick breaks in a few short minutes of high intensity. Outside of running, it's my favorite workout.

7. Plan Your Day Like You Mean It

If there was one productive habit that I would recommend over any other, it's this one. Planning your day in advance is the absolute best way to ensure you get the most value out of your time. Even with distractions that you know are coming, planning your day puts you in the driver's seat first thing in the morning and increases your odds of success by leaps and bounds.

CONNECTING THE BIG PICTURE WITH YOUR DAILY ACTIONS

With these habits in mind, think back through your grandest goals for this quarter and determine what daily habits would work best in your daily routine. Ideally, you will have healthy habits (exercise, meditation, etc.) and productive habits (those that lead directly to the achievement of your goal).

For example, if you are working toward buying a new home, you could search for new houses on the market each morning. If you are applying to graduate school, you could complete one application per day. Whatever your goal, break it down into the key habits that make the biggest long-term difference.

In the next chapter, we will be designing your ideal morning routine. This will be your chance to schedule and implement both the anchors and the resulting complementary habits that will make the biggest difference in your life and your grandest goals.

KILL THE SNOOZE BUTTON
Pitfalls, Mistakes, and Problems to Avoid

Stick to your boundaries.

Whenever we find ourselves with many great options at our disposal we tend to want to do everything—open every door, pursue every epiphany, and seize every opportunity that has presented itself.

Unfortunately, there really are only 24 hours in a day and even with so many amazing, healthy, and productive habits to adopt, neither you nor I can do it all.

This is why boundaries are essential. In addition to the 8:00 p.m. evening boundary I set for myself each night, I also set additional boundaries on a daily basis. For example, when I create my task list each morning, I create time boundaries around any vital activities that need them.

Events, meetings, and commitments involving other people tend to be the most obvious choices for boundaries. I also set time-based boundaries around my morning routine, daily workout, and meals. Whenever it's appropriate and necessary, I restrict myself with a hard deadline.

Without those restrictions I would likely chase every rabbit and follow every link that popped up. Boundaries provide structure that keep us zeroed in on the goals that need our attention while everything else is held for another day—or never.

QUICK REVIEW: ANCHOR AND COMPLEMENTARY HABITS

1. Consciously choose to form positive habits instead of accidentally letting bad habits creep into your life.

2. Ultimately, the achievement (or lack thereof) of your grandest goals is based on what you do every day.

3. Anchor habits are the core actions that you are already doing, which naturally lead to complementary habits.

4. The three core daily anchor habits are waking up with a plan, working out, and going to work.

5. The healthiest and most productive habits of high achievers include waking up early, drinking large quantities of water, prioritizing quiet time, eating a healthy breakfast, consuming positive information, working out, and planning the day in advance.

CHAPTER 6 ACTION PLAN

1. What unhealthy or unproductive personal and professional habits have you acquired over time that you would love to replace with healthy and productive habits?

1) _____

_____

2) _____

_____

3) _____

_____

2. Now, connect the big picture with your daily actions. List your most important daily habits for achieving your current grand goals.

Current Grand Goal #1:

_____

_____

Daily habits that lead directly to the achievement of this goal:

1) _____

_____

2) _____

_____

3) _____

_____

Current Grand Goal #2:

_____

_____

Daily habits that lead directly to the achievement of this goal:

1) _____

_____

2) _____

_____

3) _____

_____

Current Grand Goal #3:

_____

_____

Daily habits that lead directly to the achievement of this goal:

1) _____

_____

2) _____

_____

3) _____

_____

3. Identify when your key anchor habits and resulting complementary habits will occur, and what you must do to guarantee they will happen on a consistent basis.

Anchor Habit 1: Waking Up

Wake-up time: _____

What you must do to wake up at this time every morning:

1) _____

_____

2) _____

_____

3) _____

_____

Complementary habits that result because I wake up on time (meditation, reading, etc.):

1) _____

_____

2) _____

_____

3) _____

_____

Anchor Habit 2: Working Out

Workout time: _____

What I must do to work out consistently:

1) _____

_____

2) _____

_____

3) _____

_____

Complementary habits that result because I work out consistently (improved diet, hygiene, etc.):

1) _____

_____

2) _____

_____

3) _____

_____

Anchor Habit 3: Beginning the Day's Focused Work

Time to begin focused work: _____

What I must do to begin focused work at this time every morning:

1) _____

_____

2) _____

_____

3) _____

_____

Complementary habits that result because I get to work ready for action (improved focus, energy, etc.):

1) _____

_____

2) _____

_____

3) _____

_____

CHAPTER 7
Design Your Ideal Routines

How to Plan, Execute, and Repeat Your Best Day Ever

Routine, in an intelligent man, is a sign of ambition.

—W. H. Auden, poet

Some memories fade with time and others are so real that you can still feel the emotions as intensely as the day they happened. At this moment I can vividly feel the shivering-cold water on my face as my dad aimed a loaded squirt bottle and splashed me into reality.

That was my wake-up call on most days in high school. I had an alarm clock, but I conditioned myself to hit the snooze button and fall back asleep so fast I wouldn't remember it went off at all. So, my dad used a variety of tactics to wake me up, but the only one that still resonates at my core is that shivering-cold water. That's one way to bounce out of bed, just not quite the ideal way.

After I was jolted awake, I would make a mad dash to the bathroom, throw on a few wrinkled clothes, and shove a bowl of cereal down my throat as I ran out the door, only to drive well above the speed limit on the race to my first class. It's as though I thought school wasn't stressful enough, so I would add an extra dose of crazy to my life by reenacting a surprise hurricane evacuation drill every morning.

Years later I came to the realization that my mornings could be something more—a chance to begin my day with intention. My precious hours at sunrise evolved into a truly ideal scenario. In a short time, I discovered how to design my morning, my evening, and even my week in the best possible way.

STEP 4: YOUR IDEAL ROUTINES

So far in The 5 AM Blueprint, you have established your life's grandest goals, narrowed the list to focus on a select few in the current quarter, and identified the key anchor and complementary habits that will push you toward your goals. Now you are going to schedule the habits you chose by designing your ideal morning and evening routines, as well as your ideal week.

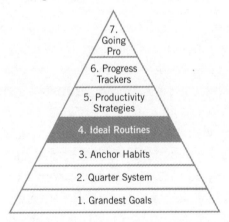

7. Going Pro
6. Progress Trackers
5. Productivity Strategies
4. Ideal Routines
3. Anchor Habits
2. Quarter System
1. Grandest Goals

HABITS, RITUALS, AND ROUTINES

Before we dive into the specifics behind your ideal schedule, let's clear up the difference between three concepts that are commonly mixed up in these kinds of discussions: habits, rituals, and routines.

As we discussed in the previous chapter, a habit is an automated and repeated action. The key to great habits, whether good or bad, is that they are hard to give up. Habits can be formed on purpose but they are not necessarily intentional when carried out. Great habits are at the core of an optimized morning routine because over time, you want your most pivotal actions to flow without a lot of conscious thought.

The more you have to think about what to do, the more likely you are to waste time between activities and even talk yourself out of doing your habits at all. Automation is the key to creating great flow in your mornings.

A ritual is a ceremony that consists of a series of actions performed according to a prescribed order. Think of a church service, wedding, or funeral.

Typically, these things are true about rituals:

1. They have a religious connotation.

2. The order of actions is consistent and cannot change.

3. There is deep meaning and purpose behind the actions.

Finally, a routine is a sequence of actions that are followed regularly, like a fixed program. For example, think of an old exercise program, driving home from work the same way each day, or buying the same type of clothes every year.

Typically, these things are true about routines:

1. There is no religious connotation.

2. The order of actions *can* change.

3. There is typically little emotion or meaning behind the actions and the activities can be lifeless or feel disconnected.

For this book, I will refer to your morning activities as a routine because I'm not going to assume any religious affiliation, the order of your morning activities can change, and it's up to you how much emotion or meaning is in place.

If you are concerned about your habits becoming too boring or lifeless, don't worry. You can always scrap your entire system and rebuild it from scratch. I do this multiple times per year as my seasons of life and priorities change. Variety is an essential ingredient and you can build that into each morning or simply change up your routine whenever it feels stale.

CREATE YOUR IDEAL WEEK

In order to dig into the specifics of your ideal morning, you need to first clearly outline the bigger picture: your ideal week. I first discovered the concept of an ideal week from Michael Hyatt, who is a master of productivity. An ideal week is based on the theory that a week could unfold nearly flawlessly from beginning to end.

That might sound farfetched, and that's the point. Your ideal week is the model to shape your life around. If you planned out your best week, including all of your major events, recurring appointments, and consistent habits, you would have a week you could (at least theoretically) repeat over and over again.

This concept is based on the idea that your weeks are fairly consistent from one to the next. If yours are not, I outline a different approach for irregular schedules later in the chapter.

The key to this process is foresight. When you proactively design what your life could look like, you are more likely to take actions that resemble that model. If you know you planned specific boundaries, healthy habits, and productive appointments throughout the week, you will certainly accomplish more of those goals over time than if you hadn't.

We are going to walk through the process of putting together your ideal week. This is your chance to imagine what your life could look like, at least from the standpoint of an idealized framework. Once again, think of this ideal week as a realistic representation of what you would normally do, but also with a touch of ambition that you may not have lived out otherwise.

1. Get Your Template

On the next page, you'll find an example of an ideal week spreadsheet based on the template available at The 5 AM Studio (http://jeffsanders.com/studio). This is meant to be altered, changed, and customized for your unique schedule.

2. Choose Your Model

There are two ideal week template models: consistent and irregular. A consistent model represents a schedule that is similar from week to week, and an irregular model represents a schedule that varies considerably from week to week.

If your schedule is fairly consistent, you can use the template above. If your schedule is irregular, you have a few options. First, you can create an ideal week based on large blocks of activity that you can reasonably depend on (sleeping, working, etc.). It would look like the consistent model, but with a lot less detail.

The second option for irregular schedules is to use a list model instead of a graphic or spreadsheet. With a list, you would simply monitor the order of events that typically happen, but without any timeframes associated with them. This model requires much more flexibility and spontaneity, but there is still ample opportunity to accomplish quite a bit each day.

The third option is to build in structure and convert your irregular schedule into a consistent one. Depending on your career and commitments, this could be more challenging, but it may be your best option to create consistency where it never existed before.

Time/Date	Mon	Tues	Wed	Thu	Fri	Sat	Sun
						IDEAL WEEK	

Time/Date	Mon	Tues	Wed	Thu	Fri	Sat	Sun
05:00–05:30	Ideal Morning routine	Ideal Morning routine	Ideal Morning routine	Ideal Morning routine	Ideal Morning routine	Sleep	Sleep
05:30–06:00							
06:00–06:30							
06:30–07:00							
07:00–07:30						Weekend Routine	Weekend Routine
07:30–08:00							
08:00–08:30							
08:30–09:00							
09:00–09:30	Priority Projects	Priority Projects	Priority Projects	Priority Projects	Priority Projects		
09:30–10:00							
10:00–10:30							
10:30–11:00							
11:00–11:30							
11:30–12:00							
12:00–12:30	Lunch	Lunch	Lunch	Lunch	Lunch		
12:30–01:00							
01:00–01:30	Projects	Projects	Projects	Projects	Projects		
01:30–02:00							
02:00–02:30							
02:30–03:00							
03:00–03:30							Weekly Review
03:30–04:00							
04:00–04:30							
04:30–05:00							
05:00–05:30	Ideal Evening Routine	Ideal Evening Routine	Ideal Evening Routine	Ideal Evening Routine	Social Event		Ideal Evening Routine
05:30–06:00							
06:00–06:30							
06:30–07:00							
07:00–07:30							
07:30–08:00							
08:00–08:30							
08:30–09:00							
09:00–09:30	sleep	sleep	sleep	sleep	sleep	sleep	sleep

Build in artificial boundaries to hold yourself to a more routine schedule. For example, you could set beginning and end times around activities that you previously left unstructured, or schedule meetings with others to reinforce a sense of urgency around your work. Find whatever means you can to make your calendar flow predictably from one week to the next.

3. Add in Your Big Rocks First

As Stephen Covey famously outlined in *The 7 Habits of Highly Effective People*, your blank schedule will fill up first with the big rocks, the nonnegotiable events, projects, and tasks that have specific timeframes. Your big rocks could include your day job, religious services, weekly piano lessons, or any other commitments that you are not giving up any time soon.

4. Fill in the Gaps with Smaller Rocks

Once the big rocks are in place, fill in the smaller rocks, the secondary priorities that typically don't have time commitments. This might include daily exercise, running errands, or other important habits you don't want to miss.

At this point, your template should be filled in completely. Any blank spots either need an associated activity or provide for a little margin. Intentionally incorporating flexibility is a great strategy because life doesn't always go as planned, even during an ideal week.

5. Review the Template Every Week

I will be discussing the weekly review process in detail in Chapter 9 (page 127). For now, plan on reviewing your ideal week template at least once a week. This will be your chance to make any necessary adjustments to keep yourself on track.

YOUR IDEAL WEEK DETERMINES YOUR DAILY ACTIONS

The timeframes that you included in your ideal week template will be your guide for your morning and evening routines. If, for example, you leave for work at 8:30 a.m. and you are planning to wake up at 6:30 a.m., then you have a two-hour window to work with for your morning routine.

Make note of how much time you have provided for your daily routines as we will use those boundaries to decide which habits you will have time for and which ones you will not.

THE FOUR TYPES OF MORNING ROUTINES

I used to operate from one well-designed morning routine that I would customize as my schedule fluctuated. Most of the time it worked out well, but it didn't take long to realize that this system was far from ideal. I went back to the drawing board and tried to figure out what was inherently wrong with my approach.

I discovered that one routine doesn't cut it—it's not flexible enough.

You need more than one routine for each of the variances in your schedule: work days, weekends, holidays, days with early-morning appointments, days when you just want to be spontaneous, and all the other random craziness that shows up in life without notice.

One routine does not account for a variable schedule or changes that pop up at the last minute. For years, on my podcast, I advocated having two different routines, one for your typical workday (when you need to be at the office by a specific time) and one for the weekend (when your schedule is more flexible). The problem is that typical workdays are not typical. Most days are different from every other.

Many people do not have to be at the office at the same time Monday through Friday, and even if they do, their schedules before and after work change all the time. We live in a fluid world, so we need a fluid schedule to bend and mold as we do, as much as we need the structure to hold everything together so life is not just a crazy conglomeration of impulsive choices.

In my attempt to solve this dilemma I created four distinct variations on an ideal morning routine, each distinguished by how much time you have available and what the rest of your day looks like. You may need more than four, depending on how many predictable variations are built into your commitments. I recommend you create a morning routine for each type of day you expect to routinely experience.

I have found that it's best to decide the night before, during your evening routine, which morning routine is best for the next day. You don't want to wake up and then decide how your morning should go. Decide ahead of time and then follow the steps you chose.

1. The Hustle

This is the fast-action routine designed for those days when you are lucky if you have time to brush your teeth. My variation of the hustle is one where I only do the bare minimum to get myself out of bed and out the door as fast as possible, which hopefully happens in under an hour. Use this routine sparingly. You don't want to get into the habit of shortening your morning routine, feeling unnecessarily stressed, and missing out on key habits.

2. The 9 to 5

This routine is the most common. This is likely the one you would use on most mornings before heading into work. My variation of the 9 to 5 lasts two to three hours and includes just enough time for a few key habits that mean the most to my day. That normally includes a few minutes of reading, a quick workout, and my favorite green smoothie.

3. The Saunter

This is a great routine for the weekend (or a non-work day) when you have all the time you want to do all of your favorite habits. You could make time for exercise, meditation, reading, taking a long walk, writing in your journal, or anything else you have missed out on recently. My variation of the saunter lasts three to five hours and this is when I normally make time for my long training runs or spending an hour or two catching up on my latest book.

4. The Custom

You may have a unique situation where your calendar doesn't match anything like what I just described. Imagine a morning where your normal routine is shaken up by a trip to the airport, sending your kids off for their first day of school, or heading to the dentist before landing at the office. On these unique mornings, create a custom routine to guarantee you are ready for what life throws at you.

DESIGN YOUR IDEAL MORNING ROUTINE

This is it! With these four variations in mind, it is now time to walk through the seven steps to design your ideal morning routine and bring your 5:00 a.m. miracle to life.

1. Get Out Your Favorite Notebook, Calendar, or Task Manager

In its simplest form, a daily routine is just a list of activities. Each morning as you go through this list, you will check off each item as you complete it. When I create my morning routines, I always begin with a list in Evernote. I perfect the list there and then I transfer it to my calendar and task manager.

Whatever system you want to use is fine; just be sure that you can easily make changes and updates to your system as needed.

2. Create Your Ideal Evening Routine

The best morning routines begin the night before. Each evening, list the order of activities you want to complete the next morning. Traditionally, the evening routine is much more flexible than the morning routine, as schedules tend to evolve more dramatically as the day progresses. However, that only makes it even more important to structure your evening routine with solid boundaries to keep your system sustainable for the long term.

Without a solid evening boundary, it's likely you will stay up later than you intend, which will lead to a lack of sleep or sleeping past your alarm. Either way, you would end up with a flawed morning routine right from the start.

There are a few key guidelines for the best evening routines. Try to incorporate these into your routine as well:

1. Have a solid time boundary to end work for the day and begin preparing for sleep.

2. Review your tasks for the following day in your calendar and task manager.

3. Put everything away, including all work-related materials and personal stuff around your house (this step is part of the Equilibrium Zero process that I will discuss on page 118 in the next chapter).

4. Set your alarm(s) for the following day (I use multiple alarms to guarantee I get up).

5. Turn off any bright visual screens (computers, phones, tablets, etc.) around one hour before bedtime.

6. Read or listen to fiction to allow your mind to transition into a more carefree state.

7. Create an ideal sleeping environment to fall asleep faster and easier (cooler temperatures, dark room, comfortable bed, etc.).

3. Align Your Morning Routine to Your Grandest Goals

In the previous chapter we discussed aligning your daily actions and habits to your grandest goals. It's likely that the best time of the day to schedule those actions is in the early morning during your routine. When you design your ideal morning routine, be sure to prioritize the habits that lead to the achievement of your grandest goals.

This is the key that makes the system turn. You could wake up early and simply choose random habits that make you feel good, but with long-term grand goals in mind, you could intentionally schedule specific actions that you have predetermined to push you directly toward your current quarterly objectives. This is the glue that holds The 5 AM Blueprint together.

For example, you could schedule an early-morning swim if you are training for a triathlon, or spend an hour studying Portuguese for your upcoming trip to Brazil. During the development of this book I scheduled blocks of time in my morning routine specifically for writing. I aligned my activities in the first few hours of my day to my most important goal.

Intentional, healthy, and productive habits that are aligned to your grandest goals and consistently executed in the early-morning hours paint the quintessential picture of dominating your day before breakfast.

4. Focus on Boosting Your Energy

The number one goal of my morning routine is to increase my energy for the day. I have many strategies to accomplish this goal, including drinking a liter of water and a double espresso, exercising, and having a large green smoothie for breakfast.

My focus on boosting energy has had a greater impact on my productivity than any other single strategy. More energy means more productivity and more productivity means more goal achievement.

5. Model Your Routine After High Achievers

Like we discussed in the previous chapter, there are healthy and productive habits that many successful people utilize. Here are two morning routines you could model yours after, including my own.

Example #1: Dean Karnazes, world-famous ultramarathon runner

1. Wake up at 3:30 a.m.

2. Run a marathon.

3. Eat breakfast with kids.

4. Take kids to school.

No joke. On an ideal day, Dean wakes up and runs a marathon. I couldn't think of a better example of dominating your day before breakfast.

Example #2: Me, a pretty normal guy

1. Wake up at 5:00 a.m.

2. Take vitamins.

3. Get dressed in my workout clothes.

4. Begin drinking 1 liter of water.

5. Feed and walk my dog Benny.

6. Open blinds in the house to let in a little sunshine.

7. Review daily schedule in my task manager.

8. Put out fires early: Check bank accounts, Inbox Zero (page 118), and website stats.

9. Meditate for 10 minutes.

10. Drink a double espresso.

11. Read for 20 minutes

12. Make a large green smoothie.

13. Focused Block of Time for 30–60 minutes: (e.g. writing, exercising, etc.).

14. Take a shower.

15. Get dressed for work.

16. Begin work on the day's most important project (around 9:00 a.m.).

Note the length of this list and the level of detail. I recommend you make your list even longer and with more detail to help get you started. Over time, you can scale back the intensity, simplify, and get even better results.

Also, my list is not time bound. This is a list of activities that I work through in order, but since I work for myself, I can schedule my work time on a flexible schedule. If your schedule requires strict time boundaries, include those with each activity.

Here is a short example of my previous morning routine based on time:

5:00 a.m. Wake up.

5:02 a.m. Take vitamins.

5:03 a.m. Get dressed in workout clothes.

5:05: a.m. Begin drinking 1 liter of water.

6. Write It All Down

Now's the time. Create your routine. You have the information, examples, and guidelines. Now, create your morning miracle.

7. Complete the Checklist

Now that you have completed your routine, put it through the gauntlet. Ask yourself these seven questions to determine if you need to make any changes.

1. Have I thoroughly thought through my morning routine?

2. Is my routine easily accessible and have I written it on paper or in digital form?

3. Is my routine ambitious, yet realistic to my life, meaning that it is not held to perfection?

4. Have I built in buffer time for unexpected events?

5. Does my routine include time for habits, projects, or tasks that are aligned to my highest priorities and grandest goals?

6. Have I structured my routine around the prevention of my common mistakes (like missing workouts late in the day)?

7. Does my routine focus on energy as one of the primary goals so the rest of the day is productive and fantastic?

KILL THE SNOOZE BUTTON
Pitfalls, Mistakes, and Problems to Avoid

Live in your reality.

Designing an ideal schedule is a double-edged sword. On one hand, you are able to put together a well-designed calendar of events, habits, and projects that push you toward your goals. On the other hand, you have a standard of excellence staring you in the face that you may never reach. The bar may seem too high and the fear of failing may paralyze you into inaction.

The goal is to design an ideal schedule on paper that meshes with your reality. Ideally, your schedule will represent the authentic *you* with all of your strengths, quirks, and mishaps included. Your best schedule will both challenge you to improve and accurately represent what you know you are going to do anyway.

For example, I would never create a schedule that encourages me to wake up any earlier than 5:00 a.m. I know from experience that I won't get up then. I also know I need much more time to get ready in the morning than the average person, mostly because I have so many healthy and productive habits I want to complete. My average morning routine takes more than three hours, so I will not be creating a 20-minute version any time soon.

Live in your reality. Create a schedule that makes sense to you, works with your current season of life, and encourages you to make the most of your time.

QUICK REVIEW: DESIGN YOUR IDEAL MORNING ROUTINE

1. Your ideal week is the framework for living out your best-case scenario. Take the time you need to create, update, and optimize this template on a regular basis.

2. Aligning the habits of your morning routine to your current grand goals is the definition of dominating your day before breakfast.

3. Design your morning routine with plenty of detail and structure in the beginning. You can always relax the system later as it becomes second nature.

4. Even though you may need more flexibility with your evening routine, design it with as much detail as your morning routine. This will ensure you stay on track each and every night.

5. There are seven questions (page 105) to ask yourself about your ideal morning routine. How did you do?

CHAPTER 7 ACTION PLAN

1. Create an ideal week template. The example provided for download in The 5 AM Studio (http://jeffsanders.com/studio) is meant to be altered, changed, and customized for your schedule.

Start with time blocks for your big rocks (work schedule, routine appointments, etc.), then fill in time blocks for your smaller rocks (morning routine, evening routine, meal breaks, etc.).

2. Begin your ideal morning routine with a highly structured and rigid plan. Map out the exact time you wake up and list each activity, in succession, that you plan to do until your workday begins. The more detail you include, the better.

My ideal morning routine:

Time: _____ Activity: _____

Time: _____ Activity: _____

Time: _____ Activity: _____

Time: _____ Activity: _____

Time: _____ Activity: _____

Time: _____ Activity: _____

Time: _____ Activity: _____

Time: _____ Activity: _____

3. Revisit your evening routine and make sure that it aligns with your new ideal morning and week. Knowing most people, this schedule will be more flexible, but it should be designed with just as much detail.

My ideal evening routine:

Time: _____ Activity: _____

Time: _____ Activity: _____

Time: _____ Activity: _____

Time: _____ Activity: _____

Time: _____ Activity: _____

Time: _____ Activity: _____

Time: _____ Activity: _____

Time: _____ Activity: _____

CHAPTER 8
Rockin' Productivity

The Strategies That Make the Biggest Difference

Out of clutter, find simplicity.
From discord, find harmony.
In the middle of difficulty lies opportunity.

—Albert Einstein

The last line of Einstein's quote, "In the middle of difficulty lies opportunity," has fundamentally changed the way I think about problems. For years I envisioned problems as nagging things to be solved instead of opportunities to be seized.

The challenges you face with your own productivity are not problems—they are distinct opportunities to not only get more things done, but to efficiently do the things that matter most.

This chapter outlines the top three productivity strategies that I have identified, tested, and optimized over the last few years. These strategies began as nagging problems in my life and then transformed into opportunities to reach my own productive potential.

I strongly encourage you to take each strategy to its respective limit. Your biggest successes will come from stretching yourself and your tools to the edge and back. Meekly attempting to implement a strategy will likely return lackluster results. Diving in head first and completely immersing yourself is the best scenario to push the boundaries of your own potential and achieve the outcomes you are hoping for.

STEP 5: PRODUCTIVITY STRATEGIES

Welcome to the fifth step of The 5 AM Blueprint, implementing the top three productivity strategies: consolidation, focus, and Equilibrium Zero.

In the previous chapter you created your ideal week, ideal morning routine, and ideal evening routine. The strategies presented in this chapter are designed to work in line with your ideal schedule and make just about everything you do more efficient.

All of these strategies can be adopted into your life, even if your daily calendar appears to be random, irregular, or downright crazy. There's a good chance you are already utilizing these strategies in some form, but as I mentioned, taking them to their full potential is where the magic happens.

Let's dive in!

STRATEGY 1: CONSOLIDATION

Attempting to manage your day with dozens of systems, note-taking tools, calendars, and Post-it notes could overwhelm even the most organized person. In order to reach an optimal state of productivity, it's best to consolidate everything in your life down to the fewest number of systems that you can.

Here are three consolidation techniques, with corresponding tools, that should amplify your productivity and take it to the next level.

Consolidate Your Tasks, Projects, and Events

Of all the tools I use, my task manager is my favorite. Essentially, a task manager is a glorified Post-it note. It is a singular tool for organizing all of your tasks, projects, and lists in your personal and professional life. Some task managers even double as calendars, communication tools, and personal assistants. Without a doubt, my task manager is the most important tool in my productive arsenal.

Whether you realize it or not, you have been using various forms of task managers for years. Whenever you make a list of things to do, book an appointment on a calendar, or prioritize your goals for the day, you are managing your tasks.

My hope is that you have not fallen into the trap of managing your daily tasks in a dozen different ways. I began that way, jotting down my grocery list on a notepad I found in the kitchen, breaking down a new marathon goal in a Word document, and scheduling an upcoming social event on my Outlook calendar at the office.

After reading David Allen's *Getting Things Done* and adopting his methodology, I consolidated all of my tasks, projects, events, lists, and random commitments into Nozbe, a singular digital task management system. Though I use and love Nozbe, there are many others to choose from (e.g. Wunderlist, OmniFocus, Apple's

Reminders app), and your organizational needs will likely vary quite a bit from mine.

The key is to find one system that you trust and dump your whole life into it, from personal tasks to work projects and everything in between. It's incredible how easy it is to organize your life when everything is in one streamlined location.

Consolidate Your Documents, Files, and Folders

When I graduated from college in 2007, I bought a big, wooden file cabinet, thinking that it would serve me well for years to come. Within a year I had transitioned to a paperless lifestyle and emptied that filing cabinet.

One of the smartest choices I made in those first few months after college was to consolidate my digital documents, files, and folders into one location. Though I have changed where those items are stored, the system has remained intact and served me very well ever since.

If you don't currently house all (and I mean *all*) of your documents, files, PDFs, scans, receipts, and other important pieces of content in one location, then I believe your whole life is about to change when you do. Having access to everything in one location gives you control like you have never had before. It also eliminates a huge amount of waste as you are able to delete duplicate files and old documents while also combining similar items together.

Some of the most popular digital filing services include Dropbox, Google Drive, and Microsoft OneDrive. I use Google Drive, but feel free to choose whichever system best fits your needs. I will also note that despite amazing search technology, digital filing services like these are the new junk closets—helpful to store huge amounts of stuff while also making it quite easy to find exactly what you need when you need it. It's also quite handy that many of these services offer great backup solutions too, so you don't end up losing your important content.

I certainly recommend you optimize a paperless lifestyle by consolidating all of your digital files and documents in one place. This will heighten the importance of creating a well-thought-out system. Take your time and organize your content as effectively as you organize your day.

Consolidate Your Articles, Notes, and Ideas

Permanently recording your *ah ha!* moments is essential when you want to remember your best thoughts and brightest ideas. There was a time long, long ago when all of our ideas were stored in paper journals inside file cabinets and memorable articles were cut out of magazines and glued into binders. Thankfully, we have evolved from those primitive times and now we have the ability to access anything of value in mere seconds.

The question, though, is whether or not you are taking advantage of your ability to effectively organize the most valuable information in your life. Yes, you can use the document filing systems we just discussed to store important documentation, but there are other ways that may work even better for you.

Every day I create, store, and access my ideas, notes, and relevant articles in Evernote. There are many alternatives to most technologies, and for Evernote, these include Microsoft OneNote, Simplenote, and even Google Drive or other similar filing systems.

I rely on Evernote for managing my grand goals and Quarter System, for storing ideas for new blog posts and podcast episodes, and among thousands of other things, for keeping track of my past accomplishments and noteworthy life moments.

Evernote is a blank slate, so you can store just about anything you want. The key is to have one system that manages the important information in your life, a system that lets you easily add new data, store it intelligently and permanently, and access it quickly.

With that kind of power you can dramatically amplify your own productivity overnight.

Another common issue is that we often find ourselves with a brilliant new idea and nowhere to easily record it. In addition to using Evernote, my phone, and even a paper notebook next to my bed for late-night inspiration, I also use AquaNotes, a waterproof notepad for my shower. As crazy as it sounds, it works really well. Though I take short showers I want to guarantee that every idea can be captured without having to rely on my memory.

After I record my new ideas on paper (physical notebook, Post-it note, AquaNotes, etc.), I then transfer those ideas into my preferred digital source (Evernote, task manager, calendar, etc.). This keeps my paperless system alive and well and minimizes the chance that I might forget or lose an idea that was originally recorded in a non-digital source.

STRATEGY 2: FOCUS LIKE YOUR HAIR IS ON FIRE

Consolidation works wonders for bringing your resources together and provides easy access to your most important materials. The next stage in the process, making tangible progress on your goals, requires a keen ability to focus on your work to the exclusion of everything else.

There are three core techniques that can make focusing on your highest priorities a staple part of your productive routine: scheduling focused blocks of time, isolating yourself from distractions, and working on one task at a time.

Schedule Focused, Uninterrupted Blocks of Time

If you take just one strategy from this book, I would hope it would be intentionally planning your day. The second would be scheduling focused, uninterrupted blocks of time to work on your grandest goals.

A focused block of time is simply a predetermined amount of time when you are able to work on an important task without being distracted. It is a powerful and effective strategy that eliminates interruptions, provides the context for high-quality work, and gives your brain the chance to dig in deep with creative thought.

The key to executing focused blocks of time is to create solid boundaries around them that cannot be crossed. This is where most people lose their way, and it's only the first step in the process. Your mission is to schedule beginning and end times around your blocks, and then guard them like the crown jewels. Think of it as scheduling an important, non-negotiable meeting with yourself. If a request for your time pops up that conflicts with your block of time, politely decline the invitation because you cannot renegotiate your commitment.

Your ideal week is the best place to turn to first when choosing the optimal times to schedule your recurring blocks. Revisit the ideal week you created in the previous chapter and determine when to schedule 90-minute blocks of time to work on your grandest goals. 90 minutes is only a suggestion, but that amount of time is usually enough to dig in deep and make significant progress on a project.

If your normal workday is typically filled with distractions, you will be amazed at how much high-quality work can be accomplished in a short time period when you are totally focused.

Isolate Yourself from Distractions

The technological boom in the last few years has morphed into an environment of nonstop communication. The pings and dings of mobile devices, flexibility of location independent jobs, and demands of 24/7 work cycles has made it more challenging now than ever to adhere to solid boundaries around your time. Because we are always connected, we are also always expected to be available at a moment's notice. During your focused blocks of time, this expectation is going to be put on hold.

Instead of being available to others, you are going to block them and yourself from anything that is not your top priority. You can best accomplish this by completely removing yourself from the environments that breed distraction.

Isolate yourself. Be alone. Run and hide. Find the best location that provides only the resources you need and nothing else. My favorite isolated place is the library. My best workdays are the ones where I bring my laptop, headphones, and snacks up to the top floor. I find a cubby in a far corner and bury myself behind a tall bookcase.

I even go so far as to turn off my phone, email program, and other unnecessary technological devices. I love social media just as much as anyone, but I often find myself checking my phone and random websites throughout the day looking for a distraction when I should be focused on my work.

What has proven to work well for me is to install website-blocking software on my computers to hold me back from doing anything other than my work. This is exactly how great habits are formed: Get a solid reminder (website blocked), go back to performing the habit (doing your work), and then experience the reward (work accomplished!).

When in doubt, do whatever you can to stay on track, even blocking Facebook from yourself.

For all intents and purposes, when I am in my isolated zone, I don't exist. No one can find me and no one can contact me. It's a magical situation. In this environment, I get more high-quality work done than in any other location on earth. For the kind of work I do, this is ideal. Your work may require a different scenario, so create it. Disconnect from the world and focus on the work that needs your full energy, focus, and attention.

Work on One Task at a Time

The third technique that can have a dramatic impact on your ability to focus is to simply choose one task to work on at a time. Once again, this may sound obvious, but think back to the scenario I just discussed when you would have to turn off so many devices to simply focus on anything, let alone just one thing.

Attempting to work on multiple tasks at a time is a losing battle because your brain functions at its best when it can put all of its resources in one direction. Multitasking is a myth and it severely impedes your ability to dig deep into a project and think creatively.

Working on just one thing can be quite the challenge, but it's often even more difficult to choose which task to focus on first. With so many priorities demanding your attention, you need a focusing mechanism to choose just the right thing to do. Gary Keller and Jay Papasan wrote a phenomenal book called *The ONE Thing* where they ask the most powerful qualifying question I have ever come across, "What's the *one* thing I can do, such that by doing it, everything else will be easier or unnecessary?"

This question is a game-changer, especially when you are in the midst of a busy work cycle and need to focus on only the few things that will make the biggest difference. This question can be applied to much more than choosing what work to do during a focused block of time, but start there. Use the power of that question to make the best decision now and move forward quickly.

Another effective filter, or way to clarify how one decision is potentially better than another, is to use a technique from Greg McKeown's phenomenal book, *Essentialism.* McKeown presents a concept that you can apply to just about any situation, "If it isn't a clear yes, then it's a clear no."

The next time you are wondering whether or not to do something, make sure the answer is undoubtedly yes. If not, keep looking until you find it.

STRATEGY 3: EQUILIBRIUM ZERO

After spending a solid workday focusing your efforts on your grandest goals, it eventually becomes time to wrap up your work and land at a clean stopping point.

I created a concept called Equilibrium Zero to house all of the strategies that have allowed me to wrap up each day in the most simplified manner possible. Equilibrium Zero is the blanket term for describing its four components: Inbox Zero, Project Management Zero, Desktop Zero, and Home Base Zero.

When you implement the concepts in Equilibrium Zero, you are able to end each day clearly acknowledging what you accomplished and with a solid foundation to build from for the next day. The term equilibrium means "a state of rest or balance due to the equal action of opposing forces." That's the goal at the end of each day, to find an optimal state of balance and peace so you can rest easy and begin the next day right where you intended.

Inbox Zero. Your inbox is not your to-do list; that's what your task manager is designed to handle. At least once a day you should reach a point where there are zero emails in your inbox. That's not 10 emails that you have already read and will respond to tomorrow—this literally means zero emails because you have already properly processed every message that arrived in the last 24 hours.

If your inbox is out of control, this is your chance to clean it up for good using a concept called Inbox Zero that was created by productivity expect Merlin Mann. First, schedule one focused block of time (or more if you need it) to get your inbox fully emptied. Second, schedule a time each day to process all of your messages.

How to process your email:

1. Delete or file all spam, junk mail, and messages that do not require a reply.

2. Reply to the messages that require a quick or reasonable response time, and then delete or file those messages.

3. If a message requires significant effort, further research, or is a task itself, reply back to the sender and tell them when you will provide a full response. Then, schedule that task in your task manager and file the email in a separate folder outside of your inbox.

4. Repeat steps 1 through 3 over and over again until your inbox is empty.

How to prevent email buildup:

1. Unsubscribe from all unneeded newsletters.

2. Communicate with your team and let them know that Inbox Zero is a priority to you. It's best when everyone adheres to this policy as it cuts down on unneeded emails being sent in the first place.

3. Schedule time each day to process email and stick to Inbox Zero once every 24 hours.

4. Schedule focused blocks of time to catch up on emails if you get behind.

If you have too many emails to handle yourself, consider restructuring your work schedule to manage your email or even hiring an assistant to filter and process emails for you.

Communicating quickly and effectively is a critical tool for enhanced productivity. When you adhere to Inbox Zero you see a dramatic improvement in the pace at which you complete tasks and projects, not to mention the respect from those who are communicating with you.

Project Management Zero. There's not much I hate worse than going to bed with an unfinished task on my mind. In order to prevent this from happening, I started a daily practice of only scheduling my highest-priority tasks and ensuring it was reasonable to complete those tasks before the day was over.

The concept of Project Management Zero simply refers to your commitment to fully finish a task or project before moving on to the next one. I've already discussed that it is best to work on one task at a time and avoid multitasking. With Project Management Zero, you will focus on one aspect of a project at a time while not trying to juggle too many items at once.

The tendency for most is to get distracted or excited about an upcoming task. We often find ourselves starting many things, but finishing nothing. Make it your priority to completely finish what you are working on before you make any moves toward your future goals. Utilize your task manager or note-taking system to create a list for all of those great future ideas.

At the end of each day, find a clean stopping point on your current project by finishing the task you are working on and scheduling the next task for the next most appropriate time slot.

Desktop Zero. Think of your desktop as your email inbox; it should be totally clear by the end of the day. The difference between Inbox Zero and Desktop Zero is that your desk will likely have a few key items on it that are supposed to be there all the time (e.g. computer, keyboard, mouse, lamp, etc.).

The desk I use in my home office has a select few items on it, and those items remain there regardless of what projects I am working on at the time. However, at the end of each task, and especially at the end of each day, I clear the open space where random project materials end up.

Because of this practice, my desk is clean and organized 99 percent of the time. The other 1 percent is the rare moment I have many materials on it, but those are cleared away quickly and efficiently before I move on to my next task at hand.

Adhering to Desktop Zero is the same as making your bed. There is a specific look that is clean, organized, and attractive to the eye. Your goal is to achieve that look 99 percent of the time, or at least once a day.

Home Base Zero. Much like Desktop Zero, Home Base Zero is the commitment to clear the unneeded items from your home and office at the end of each day. Whether you realize it or not, everything has an ideal and organized place where it belongs. Home Base Zero challenges you to identify that specific location for every item you own or use.

At the office you may have files, folders, office supplies, furniture, or other project materials that ideally will end up stored in a cabinet, drawer, or another organizing system. At home you may have kitchen appliances, children's toys, clothing, and other household items that all belong somewhere very specific.

On an ideal day, you would head off to bed knowing that every single item you own has been put away exactly where it belongs. When this happens, you have an incredibly clean and organized environment from which you can begin your projects the very next morning. This may sound like a pipe dream, but this is possible to achieve and it is a glorious way to live day-to-day.

BRINGING IT ALL TOGETHER

To summarize what we have covered so far, think of it this way:

Imagine you begin your day (bright and early) by waking up to your task manager (Nozbe), which outlines today's workout and meditation practice (healthy habits), as well as your highest-priority tasks (part of your ideal morning routine). You begin your first focused block of time for the day (working on one of this quarter's grand goals) by accessing the important documents you need in your digital filing system (Google Drive).

Halfway through your focused block, you record a few new ideas in your online notebook (Evernote). After repeating this process a few times throughout the day, you wrap up by answering all of your emails (Inbox Zero), completing your unfinished tasks (Project Management Zero), clearing your desk (Desktop Zero), and putting away all of your project materials at home and in the office (Home Base Zero). The day comes to a close as you review your tasks for the next day and spend a few minutes with your favorite book (part of your ideal evening routine).

With the combination of clearly articulated grand goals, a focused Quarter System, properly aligned healthy habits, an ideal week, ideal morning routine, ideal evening routine, and these highly effective productivity strategies of consolidation, focused blocks of time, and Equilibrium Zero, I'm not sure how you wouldn't completely dominate your day.

But wait—there's more!

In the next two chapters, I will outline how to monitor your progress through strategic review systems, accountability meetings, and the all-important daily trackers, as well as introduce advanced strategies to optimize The 5 AM Blueprint system in its entirety.

KILL THE SNOOZE BUTTON
Pitfalls, Mistakes, and Problems to Avoid

More is not always better.

I know that I am throwing a lot at you in this book, so I'll go ahead and let you off the hook. You don't have to do everything.

In fact, as with most things in life, building off the fundamentals is the only strategy you will ever need. *More* may not be the solution at all. In the world of productivity there will always be more strategies to implement, ideas to investigate, apps to download, conferences to attend, and books to buy.

At the end of this book, I will be outlining an action plan to guide you through the process of implementing every idea I present in these chapters. It's up to you to decide which of the strategies you ultimately adopt and I will be the first to tell you that you probably only need a couple of them.

Sure, my life is based off of these principles, tools, and strategies, but I only reached this point after years of experimentation and customization. Though I exert quite a bit of effort tinkering with the tiny details to squeeze the most out of each day, I always come back to a few fundamentals that make the biggest difference.

The true goal of this book is for you to find your fundamentals and stick to them. They will be your guiding light whenever the chaos gets too intense and the demands of life are knocking loudly at your door.

In the end, simplicity wins.

QUICK REVIEW: THE PRODUCTIVITY STRATEGIES

1. Consolidating everything into a few systems is the best way to see your whole life at a glance, make adjustments, and move forward with greater efficiency.

2. Working in focused blocks of time is the smartest strategy for doing better work faster.

3. Maintaining Equilibrium Zero across all spectrums of your life ensures that you wrap up all of your projects, emails, and clutter, providing a clean space and a clear head.

4. When you bring all of the strategies together you can truly dominate your day.

CHAPTER 8 ACTION PLAN

1. Consolidate your life's goals (personal and professional), events, projects, and tasks into the fewest locations possible.

Your dedicated task manager (Nozbe, Wunderlist, OmniFocus, etc.):

_____

Date when you will consolidate (or clean up) your tasks in this system:

_____

Your calendar application (Apple Calendar, Outlook, Google Calendar, etc.):

_____

Date when you will consolidate (or clean up) your events in this system:

_____

Your online document filing system (Dropbox, Google Drive, OneDrive, etc.):

_____

Date when you will consolidate (or clean up) your files in this system:

_____

Your online research and note-taking System (Evernote, OneNote, Simplenote, etc.):

_____

Date when you will consolidate (or clean up) your notes in this system:

_____

2. When are you most productive? Schedule and guard focused blocks of time around your most important daily goals.

Grand goal #1:

_____

Location and focused block of time each day/week when you will work on this goal:

_____

Grand goal #2:

_____

Location and focused block of time each day/week when you will work on this goal:

_____

Grand goal #3:

_____

Location and focused block of time each day/week when you will work on this goal:

_____

3. Implement Equilibrium Zero once every 24 hours (Inbox Zero, Project Management Zero, Desktop Zero, and Home Base Zero). Also create a daily reminder in your task manager to get to zero in each of these areas every day.

Date when you will clear your current inbox to zero emails:

_____

Time each day that you will get to Inbox Zero:

_____

Date when you will get your current grand goal to zero partially completed tasks:

_____

Time each day that you will get to Project Management Zero:

_____

Date when you will clear off your desk to the bare essentials:

_____

Time each day that you will get to Desktop Zero:

_____

Date when you will clean up your home and office, leaving out only what's needed:

_____

Time each day that you will get to Home Base Zero:

_____

CHAPTER 9
Tracking Bold Progress

How to Monitor, Measure, and Manage Your Ambitious Life

Unhappy people are not in control of their lives because they spend their days coping with the random bad results of unmanaged systems. Happy people are in control of their lives, spending their days enjoying the intentional good results of managed systems.

—Sam Carpenter, author of *Work the System*

I am confident that one of the only reasons I did well in school was because of the syllabus handed out on the first day of class. That magical document was the framework for every assignment, test, and scheduled activity for the entire semester.

One of my favorite college professors, Dr. Jeffrey Vittengl, was a master of the syllabus. His level of detail and clarity was unrivaled and it was nearly impossible to not do well in his class unless you literally did nothing.

Don't get me wrong, his classes were not easy—but the expectations were crystal clear. There was no ambiguity or confusion; there were no contradictions. He had a keen ability to map out how each step of the class would progress, and he would review the steps with each of us along the way.

With that kind of pristine plan in place and the benchmarks to keep every student on track, success was unavoidable. That's an ideal scenario and it's one you can duplicate with your own goals every quarter.

All you need is the right review systems to hold yourself accountable and to keep all of the moving parts flowing in the same direction.

STEP 6: TRACKING BOLD PROGRESS

The sixth step of The 5 AM Blueprint is tracking your progress. Once you discover how to dominate one day before breakfast, the key is then to be able to repeat that process over and over again without getting off track.

The review systems outlined in this chapter will show you how to monitor, measure, and maintain your amazing productivity for the long term.

The indispensable review systems that will keep your goals on schedule for completion include a daily review, weekly review, monthly review, quarterly review, and annual review. We will also discuss how to maintain the corresponding tracking documents and how to set up an effective meeting with an accountability partner to monitor your progress at each interval.

DAILY REVIEW

You have many options when it comes to tracking your daily tasks and accomplishments. I certainly recommend you maintain a task manager and a calendar system to know what to do and when, but it is also imperative that you can look back at the end of each day to see what actually got done.

When it comes to daily tracking, the best system for you is the one you will actually use. I will show you how to use the old school tracking document that works for me, but feel free to use any apps, spreadsheets, or effective methods like the Seinfeld Strategy.

Jerry Seinfeld, the comedian, is well known for a habit-forming method built around writing jokes every day. After his daily joke-writing session, he would mark a big red X on a physical paper calendar. His only goal was to mark an X every day and not break the streak. The simple motivation to keep the streak alive kept him returning day after day to write more jokes.

NOTE: I have been personally using and discussing the Seinfeld Strategy for years, but while conducting research for this book, I discovered that Seinfeld did not create this method and never actually used it himself. He loves receiving credit for its creation, though no one is quite sure who developed it.

Nonetheless, since the method is powerful and effective, it is still a great strategy to add to your productivity arsenal.

You can call this your Daily Rituals and Habits Tracker. This simple spreadsheet is a daily reminder of the core habits in your life that are aligned to your grandest goals.

Daily Rituals and Habits Tracker										
Week	M	T	W	T	F	S	S	Done	Goal	Net
Wake up @ 5 am	1	1	1	1	1			5	5	0
Meditate 10 min	2	1		1		1	1	6	7	−1
Drink 1 liter water	2		1	2		1		7	7	−1
Run 2 miles	1			1	1		1	4	5	−1
Read 30 min	1	1	1	1		1	1	6	6	0
							Total	27	30	−3

Follow these steps to set up your own habits tracker:

1. Adjust this week's date in the top left corner of the tracker. I recommend you duplicate this spreadsheet every week and keep track of your quarterly progress in one document.

2. Replace the habits in the left column with your core daily habits. Be very specific. Notice how I included the exact time to wake up, the number of minutes to meditate, and the precise amount of water to drink.

3. Update the "goal" column with the number of repetitions you plan to execute each week. Each habit can have a different weekly goal. Keep this number ambitious, yet realistic.

4. Choose a specific time each day to update your tracker with the number of repetitions you performed. Many people find it works best to update the tracker as part of their ideal evening routine.

At the end of each week, during your weekly review, you will have the chance to review your weekly progress and make adjustments for the upcoming week.

WEEKLY REVIEW

After intentionally planning your day and scheduling focused blocks of time for your grandest goals, completing a weekly review is the next most effective strategy that you cannot skip.

When you successfully complete a weekly review (even once), you will gain enormous clarity over your entire schedule, all of the tasks on your plate, the habits you care about, and the commitments you have made.

Weekly Review (January 1–7, 2016)	
Wins and Accomplishments	
1	
2	
3	
Losses	
1	
2	
3	
Fixes	
1	
2	
3	

A weekly review is not complicated, and it should not require a large amount of your time, maybe one or two hours a week; however, the benefits are staggering.

Before I implemented a formal weekly review process, I was reasonably productive. I thought I knew what was going on most of the time and I stayed on track fairly well. After I began systematically reviewing my tasks, projects, events, goals, and commitments, I dramatically improved my output and focus.

The weekly review process forces you to ask simple but direct questions, schedule the tasks that matter more than any other, and make the necessary adjustments to continue pushing directly toward your end results.

Clear a few hours on your schedule once a week to complete the following steps. It can be done anytime, as long as it is consistent.

1. Review your ideal week template (page 96). Ensure that the framework for the big picture is intact and accurately represents your life right now.

2. Review the habits you included in your Daily Rituals and Habits Tracker. Add, remove, or modify your habits to keep them ambitious and aligned to your current goals.

3. Update your progress reports in your goals notebook (as discussed in Chapter 5, page 69). Write down what you accomplished last week and clearly note what your next actions will be for the upcoming week for each of your quarterly grand goals.

4. Complete your weekly review document (create your own, or download a copy of the example provided here from The 5 AM Studio at JeffSanders.com/studio). Answer each of the questions and take your time to reflect on the previous week.

5. Post your Top 3 Goals of the week somewhere you will see them often. I have a vision board hanging in my home office where I write out my weekly goals on a large Post-it note. This acts as a constant reminder to stay focused on what matters.

6. Schedule your Top 3 Goals in your task manager and calendar. This is when you will schedule your focused blocks of time for the week and use those blocks to work on your top weekly goals. Rearrange your other commitments around these blocks.

7. Review all of your upcoming tasks, events, projects, and commitments for the next few weeks. The more time you spend planning, the less time you waste in execution. Review as much as you need to in order to feel confident about your calendar. If you are at all unsure about your schedule, go back and plan some more.

For my own weekly review, I created a recurring task in my task manager that lists each of these steps in a checklist format. Every Sunday night I go through the checklist and complete each step just in time for my Monday morning accountability call.

WEEKLY ACCOUNTABILITY MEETINGS

My friend Matt Frazier runs an amazing website called No Meat Athlete (NoMeatAthlete.com). For years I followed him online and after I had the opportunity to interview him for my podcast, he invited me to be his accountability partner.

Up until that time I had never worked with someone one-on-one for the sole reason of holding each other accountable to our own goals. After a few weeks of customizing how we wanted to structure this working relationship, we had a great thing going.

Accountability sounds like something that happens to irresponsible people who do bad things. Even the phase, "being held accountable," implies that you cannot manage your own responsibilities and a third party has to come in and force you to do your work.

What I discovered with Matt was quite the opposite. Accountability has everything to do with exerting a little outside pressure to keep you on your toes. It's not about being guilted into doing your work, but rather having the opportunity to discuss your progress with a close friend.

I will admit that knowing I will be discussing my progress with Matt on Monday provides great motivation to complete any unfinished work on Sunday.

Matt lives in Asheville, North Carolina, and I live in Nashville, Tennessee, so every Monday morning we host a 30-minute video chat through Skype. During that time, we review quite a few topics. Here's the breakdown of our typical weekly accountability meeting.

Wins and accomplishments. What three things went really well last week? What are you proud of? Did anything new and surprising happen?

Losses. What did not go well? Where did you drop the ball? What goals did you fail to achieve?

Fixes. How will you correct the problems from last week? Specifically, what do you plan to do this week to make sure the problems do not return?

Ah ha! moments: What brilliant insights did you come across? What new ideas are you excited about? Did you find anything inspirational or reflective while reading, attending a seminar, or talking to a friend?

Goals for the week. What are your top three goals for next week? What are you willing to commit to achieving?

Personal development materials. How will you enrich yourself this week? What books are you reading? What workshops are you attending? What audio programs, podcasts, or audio books will you be listening to?

Skills to practice. How will you get better at what you do? What skill sets are you sharpening? What new skills will you be developing?

Technically, you don't need an accountability partner. After all, you could simply complete your weekly review process alone and accomplish the same amount of work. However, I highly recommend you find someone in a similar season of life to share your goals with each week.

It is a surprisingly wonderful experience to have the chance to bounce ideas off one another, and you will likely make more progress as a team than you ever would on your own.

Another key teamwork strategy is to surround yourself with brilliant individuals in a mastermind group. This is a surefire way to achieve success faster and on a bigger scale than you could have reached on your own. Mastermind groups are phenomenal excuses for getting together with a bunch of smart, ambitious, and helpful people who all want to help each other succeed.

My experience with mastermind groups has proven that we are all better off together than on our own. Find a group or create your own. Just make it a priority to meet regularly with people who support you and your grandest goals.

MONTHLY REVIEW

Each month marks the end of one third of a quarter, which makes it a logical place to pause and review your progress thus far. The monthly review process is very similar to the weekly review, but with slightly different questions to appeal to the bigger picture.

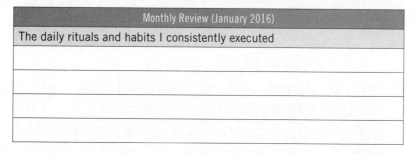

Monthly Review (January 2016)
The daily rituals and habits I consistently executed

The daily rituals and habits that need improvement

What I will do next month to be more consistent

Wins and accomplishments

Follow these steps to complete your monthly review process:

1. Review your habits from the Daily Rituals and Habits Tracker (page 130). Which habits did you consistently execute throughout the month? What worked well for you? What habits were the most inconsistent? What prevented you from staying consistent with these habits?

2. Review your progress reports in your goals notebook. Are you on track to complete this goal by the end of the quarter? If necessary, what changes need to be made to get back on track?

3. Complete your monthly review document (create your own, or download a copy of the example provided here from The 5 AM Studio at JeffSanders.com/studio). It helps to refer to your previously completed weekly review documents to answer each question.

4. Choose three goals to be your top three for the next month. These will likely be the three most important tasks from your current quarterly goals.

5. Review all of your upcoming tasks, events, projects, and commitments for the next month. Make note of any major obstacles coming up, including travel, conferences, parties, meetings, or other major events that could derail your normal schedule.

Hold on to your Monthly Review documents. You will need each of them to complete your quarterly reviews.

QUARTERLY REVIEW

The quarterly review marks the end of a major milestone. Ideally, at this point you would have successfully completed the grand goals you began at the beginning of the quarter.

During the review, you will reflect back and see if your grand vision held true for the last 90 days. If not, you have your work cut out for you next quarter.

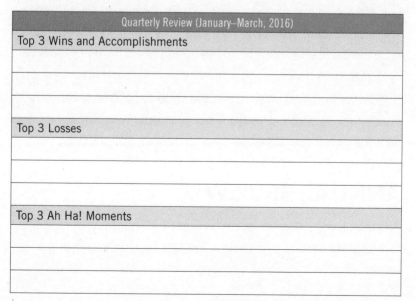

Quarterly Review (January–March, 2016)
Top 3 Wins and Accomplishments
Top 3 Losses
Top 3 Ah Ha! Moments

Follow these steps to complete your quarterly review process:

1. Update your habits from the Daily Rituals and Habits Tracker. These habits should have reflected your goals from the previous quarter and now they may need an update to reflect your goals for the next quarter.

2. Complete your progress reports in your goals notebook. Ideally, at this point you will be wrapping up your grandest goals for the quarter and reflecting back on the progress you made.

3. Complete your quarterly review document (create your own or download a copy of the example provided here from The 5 AM Studio at JeffSanders.com/studio). It helps to refer to your previously completed monthly review documents to answer each question.

4. Choose the grandest goals you will be pursuing in the next quarter. Also, create your new plan for each goal in your digital notebook (Evernote) and then set up the respective next actions list (page 68) and progress reports.

5. Review all of your upcoming tasks, events, projects, and commitments for the next quarter. Plan ahead now for all of the focused blocks of time you will need for this quarter's grandest goals.

The end of a quarter is a great time for a break or even an offsite visit to a cabin in the woods. Planning your life requires solitude and focus. Take the time you need and plan well.

ANNUAL REVIEW

Assuming you have adopted the Quarter System and completed thorough quarterly reviews for the last four quarters, you might assume that you really don't need to do an annual review.

However, I have found it to be very valuable to look back at the big picture of my life over the last few quarters to see how my goals have turned out.

2016 Annual Review
Top 3 Wins and Accomplishments
Top 3 Losses
Top 3 Ah Ha! Moments

Here are a few questions to answer once every 12 months:

1. What were your most consistent habits last year? What lessons can you glean from those successes to help form the habits that never quite stuck?

2. What major milestones did you reach last year? What grand goals were accomplished? How much better is your life now than it was one year ago today?

3. How well does the Quarter System work for you? Should your goals be scheduled on a different timeframe, like 60 days instead of 90, or 6 months instead of 3?

4. Complete your annual review document (complete your own or download a copy of the example provided here from The 5 AM Studio at JeffSanders.com/studio). It helps

to refer to your previously completed quarterly review documents to answer each question.

5. Revisit your grandest goals list and start fresh. In an ideal world, what ridiculous, amazing, and mind-blowing adventures would you embark on?

As cliché as it is, the end of a calendar year is a great time to pause, reflect, and plan to begin again. Take the time to process the practical changes that will make a real difference in the near future.

KILL THE SNOOZE BUTTON
Pitfalls, Mistakes, and Problems to Avoid

Know when to ditch your own goals.

When an opportunity appears out of nowhere, how do you know if you should take it?

The more ambitious, productive, and high-achieving you are, the more likely you will find yourself with opportunities you never saw coming. I never expected to write this book. I was presented with the chance to do so out of the blue.

When I was contacted by my publisher with an offer to write the book, I was in the middle of two big business projects and in the beginning stages of buying my first house.

I was busy.

What made this decision easy was the clarity I had around my quarterly goals at the time. Because I had spent each and every week reviewing my projects, I knew where I stood. I knew the progress I had made, what tasks were coming up next, and how those tasks stacked up against my plans for the next few months.

In other words, I had been working hard on increasing my own self-awareness around my grandest goals, current projects, and ever-changing schedule. So, when I compared writing a book with my schedule at the time, the choice was clear.

It's not always that easy to make those kinds of decisions. However, the more you know about where you stand with your current goals, the easier it is to know when it's time to ditch them for something even better.

QUICK REVIEW: TRACKING BOLD PROGRESS

1. You are responsible for tracking your own goals and staying focused on what matters most. With the right review systems in place, this can be a breeze.

2. The weekly review process is the most important tracking tool. It is your chance to pause, get a big-picture perspective on your progress, and then dive back in with a clear plan for the next seven days.

3. A great accountability partner can make the difference between following through on your goals and letting yourself off the hook. Finding someone you trust to discuss your life with provides a phenomenal opportunity to stay true to your plan and not veer too far off course.

CHAPTER 9 ACTION PLAN

1. Update your Daily Rituals and Habits Tracker each day.

Time each day that you will update your Daily Rituals and Habits Tracker:

---

2. Brainstorm two or three people who could become your accountability partner. Then, plan to meet with each one to determine if the two of you would make a good fit.

People you will meet with to discuss creating an accountability partnership:

_____

_____

_____

3. Create or download and then complete the templates for your daily, weekly, monthly, quarterly, and annual reviews. Schedule time on your calendar every week for the review. Friday afternoons and Sunday evenings are the most popular times. If possible, meet with your accountability partner soon after you finish your review each week.

Weekly day and time you will complete your weekly review (usually takes 1 to 2 hours):

_____

Weekly day and time you will meet with your accountability partner:

_____

During your *weekly* review, you will complete the following:

1) _____

2) _____

3) _____

4) _____

5) _____

During your *weekly* meeting with your accountability partner, you will discuss:

1) _____

2) _____

3) _____

4) _____

5) _____

During your *monthly* review, you will complete the following:

1) _____

2) _____

3) _____

4) _____

5) _____

During your *quarterly* review, you will complete the following:

1) _____

2) _____

3) _____

4) _____

5) _____

During your *annual* review, you will complete the following:

1) _____

2) _____

3) _____

4) _____

5) _____

CHAPTER 10
The 5 AM Professional

Advanced Strategies for the High Achiever Who Wants It All

Without ambition one starts nothing. Without work one finishes nothing. The prize will not be sent to you. You have to win it.

—Ralph Waldo Emerson

I had a profound experience a few years ago while reading Steven Pressfield's book *Turning Pro*. In that short but powerful book, Pressfield describes the subtle shift that takes place when you move from the life of an amateur to the life of a professional. It is a dramatic transition, though at its core, it is merely an act of will.

Being a true professional implies that you are no longer willing to do what amateurs do. Amateurs do things when they feel like it instead of when those things need to be done; amateurs hope they will be successful instead of working directly for the success they desire; and amateurs work part-time on their dream instead of full-time on their clear and ambitious goals.

As Pressfield writes, "[Turning pro] changes our days completely. It changes what time we get up and it changes what time we go to bed. It changes what we do and what we don't do. It changes the activities we engage in and with what attitude we engage in them. It changes what we read and what we eat. It changes the shape of our bodies. When we were amateurs, our life was about drama, about denial, and about distraction. Our days were simultaneously full to the bursting point and achingly, heartbreakingly empty. But we are not amateurs any more. We are different, and everyone in our lives sees it."

To become a 5:00 a.m. pro, you must let go of your amateur status and enter the world of intentional success. 5:00 a.m. pros wake up when they plan to wake up. They know what they want and they have a detailed plan in place to see it through. 5:00 a.m. pros implement healthy habits and strategically choose each and every aspect of their day knowing just how important each and every day can be.

To call yourself a 5:00 a.m. pro, you will not need my approval, or to cross any predetermined finish lines. All you need is an act of will, a simple decision right here and now to prioritize your grandest goals and to pursue them with gusto.

And sure, waking up at 5:00 a.m. would certainly help, but that's just my opinion.

STEP 7: ADVANCED STRATEGIES

Welcome to the seventh and final step of The 5 AM Blueprint. This chapter outlines the top five advanced strategies that are designed to work with and optimize the concepts in The 5 AM Blueprint.

Assuming you have a great handle on your own morning routine, productivity system, and healthy habits, these strategies can supplement your work and enhance your progress. Like many advanced strategies, these techniques work best when you are already in a productive flow and simply want to get even better.

Throughout my own journey of enhanced productivity I have found all of these strategies to be just what I needed to take my progress to the next level and truly be the icing on the cake.

Though I personally use and love each of the strategies, don't feel obligated to adopt all of them. It may be tempting to want to dive in head first, but hold off on overwhelming yourself right now. There's plenty of time for that later.

SCHEDULE TIME FOR THINKING

You become what you think about. We all do. What we think about determines our goals, our attitudes, and our ultimate achievements.

In the beginning of my own personal development journey, I discovered one of the greatest (and most obvious) strategies in existence, and it has transformed not only how I think, but also what I now choose to think about. This simple strategy is to schedule time just for thinking.

Earl Nightingale, the late pioneer of the modern personal development industry, created an audio program called *Lead the Field*. This is where I first discovered this powerful thinking strategy.

Scheduling time just for thinking is a highly underutilized productivity strategy, especially for busy people. It seems so obvious because it sounds just like brainstorming, but it's much more than that.

To make the most of this strategy, schedule a focused block of time, isolate yourself, bring your favorite notebook, whiteboard, or journal, and ask yourself one vitally important life question. Write that question at the top of your writing space and then spend up to an hour brainstorming and recording as many answers to this question as you can.

The key is to ask yourself tough questions, especially ones regarding your current grand goals. What you will soon discover is that breakthroughs are imminent. You will inevitably land on brilliant ideas and experience triumphant *ah ha!* moments that can push your goals forward faster than by simply checking items off a to-do list.

Also, the more often you give your brain the space to think about tough problems the more creative and brilliant you will be. Schedule at least a few thinking sessions per week to optimize this strategy.

In *Lead the Field,* Earl outlines when to think: "Pick one hour a day that you can count on fairly regularly. The best time for me is an hour before the others are up in the morning. The mind is clear, the house is quiet, and if you like, with a fresh cup of coffee, this is the time to start the mind going."

You see what this means? Even decades ago the 5:00 a.m. miracle was alive and well, and successful individuals like Earl Nightingale were making the most of it!

Of all the advanced strategies a 5 a.m. professional could choose from, this one trumps them all. Schedule consistent time for thinking and you will undoubtedly find a way to achieve whatever you set your mind to.

MUSIC DESIGNED FOR FOCUS

I spend many hours every day *attempting* to work. Whether or not I actually get anything done has a lot to do with how well I cut distractions and focus on what matters.

One strategy that has revolutionized how I get work done is listening to music designed for my brain. I use a service called Focus@Will that creates music tracks based on neuroscience. Though I cannot explain the science (and you're lucky that I am not even going to try), the positive and productive effects are easy to notice.

I spend as many as 10 to 12 hours a day in front of a computer and much of that time involves me wearing headphones and listening to Focus@Will's *Up Tempo* station at a high-energy music level. What I experience is nothing short of a flow state, or getting "in the zone." Within a few moments the music fades away and I laser in on my work.

The music tracks from Focus@Will are designed to help you focus, reduce distractions, improve your attention span, and learn considerably more while you work. I find that it's best to use music like this when reading, writing, studying, or doing hardcore mental activity.

Prior to Focus@Will, I listened to techno or house music and it had a similar effect, though what I use now is certainly better because it is easier to forget about the music and think about the task at hand. What this means for you is that there is a type of music that is best for your brain and your ability to focus.

Music is a powerful force on your attention and finding your ideal music is important if you want to repeatedly achieve your ideal workflow.

STANDING DESK

Being more physically active is the name of the game when it comes to increased energy, productivity, and better health. One of my all-time favorite strategies for just those reasons is using a standing desk.

I have been standing all day for years and it has made a tremendous difference in my productivity, posture, digestion, energy, attitude, and willingness to keep working long after I normally would have stopped.

It's also incredibly important to incorporate standing, walking, and more movement in general throughout your normal workday to prevent a myriad of health problems that accompany stagnation, including higher rates of cardiovascular disease, increased obesity, and a higher probability of an early death.

If you are used to sitting at a desk for eight hours a day, standing can dramatically improve your health and how much you get done.

You have two options to get your first standing desk up and ready: buy one or build one. I highly recommend you build your first desk with materials you already have available so you won't have to spend a dime and so you will have time to experiment with standing more before you invest in anything.

I put together my first standing desk by stacking old textbooks on top of my current desk, so don't presume you have to spend any money to get the benefits I am describing.

Once you have committed to a standing desk you can buy higher-end models or custom build your own to suit your needs. My current standing desk is a custom-built wooden desk that is fashioned on top of my previous desk. It's not pretty, but it works wonders.

Adjusting to a standing desk can take a week or two, depending on your current fitness level. Your back will be sore, so slowly build up to standing all day. It's helpful to incorporate other fitness activities to strengthen your back while you make this transition. I also highly recommend you buy a cushioned mat to stand on because you will likely need the extra support. High-quality standing mats are cheap and can be found online easily.

Start standing now and feel the difference.

THE NEW VISION BOARD

Vision boards are a physical display of things you want, usually hung on the wall on a cork board with pictures of houses, cars, or other similar items that are cut out from magazines. Essentially, this is an old school model of envisioning your life by idealizing the end result.

This method doesn't work. It's great to begin with the end in mind, but there's more to it than that. Visualization is only the first step and, without a strategy, it gets you nowhere.

I recommend you start with this old school method to gain clarity over what you are trying to achieve. Then, advance to the *new* vision board, which is a representation of the journey. It focuses on the processes and work that lead to end results and outcomes you want.

For example, you could include an image of running at sunrise as an action that leads to a marathon, or writing in a coffee shop on your way to publishing your first book.

Old school vision boards never worked for me because I would always post pictures of fancy cars, even though I am not motivated by cars at all. Posting potentially inspiring images of a life you don't have often leads to guilt around your lack of progress. Instead, focus on the process to get there.

The best vision boards answer the question, *how will I get to my goal?* Without the *how,* you only have the *what*, and the *what* is never enough.

The new vision board uses pictures, images, quotes, and practical reminders of what you will be doing all along the way to get to your grand goal. It's that simple.

Practical vision boards like this new model I am describing have many benefits, including focusing on the actions you can take, preventing you from being distracted by distant fantasies, and encouraging you to take control of your future with specific habits today.

To create your new vision board, buy a corkboard or find a blank wall in your house to pin things to. Referring to your list of grand goals, focus exclusively on your current quarterly objectives and write detailed descriptions of the process to achieve each goal. Then find images, quotes, or inspirational content that directly reflect a few of the key steps in each action plan.

Revisit your vision board at least once a quarter and update it as needed. With a well-thought-out plan in place, your vision board can act as a phenomenal reminder to keep you focused on what matters most right now.

INVERSION

This may be the most bizarre advanced strategy in the group, but trust me when I say this is going to flip your perspective on going pro. Inversion, or hanging upside down, can actually improve your health and help you get more done.

I was first convinced to try out inversion after watching a series of videos, many of them from Dr. Robert Lockhart, an Australian physician who has been practicing inversion on a daily basis for more than 40 years.

The goal behind inversion is to reverse the effects of gravity. Gravitational forces are hard on the body and when you reverse gravity you relieve incredible amounts of pressure and disrupt your normal rhythms, which carries with it benefits you cannot get with any other exercise.

Other benefits include a significant reduction in back pain, less stress, better brain functioning with an increased flow of blood to your head (which helps productivity), improved leg and core strength, better joint health, improved flexibility, better posture, clearer skin, reduced wrinkles, an improved lymphatic system, and from my personal experience, the ability to grow taller.

Inversion is not a miracle cure for everyone and there are a few potential drawbacks, including the fact that hanging upside down can be hard on your joints, it takes a while to get used to, it could be dangerous to practice alone, and the inversion equipment is a little bulky and difficult to store.

I have been inverting nearly every day for over a year and from my experience (and despite the potential drawbacks), this is a phenomenal practice for anyone in decent physical shape who wants the benefits I just described. Within a few weeks of beginning this practice, I noticed less back pain and improved mental clarity, and I was actually 1/8 of an inch taller! Not much, but it's progress.

You can practice inversion with a pair of gravity boots, an inversion chair, or an inversion table. I invert every day with gravity boots for 10 minutes after my daily run, and it is my favorite way to cap off a great workout.

Hanging upside down is a bizarre way to spend your time, but I continue to find it incredibly beneficial. You can even combine inversion with other healthy habits at the same time, like meditation, affirmations, crunches, squats, and listening to a great podcast.

There's a lot you can do while just hanging around!

Work Hard. Play Hard.

The results of one of my podcast audience surveys revealed that most people want a life where they work hard and then play hard. Most noted that they did not want a life of mediocrity, sameness, or consistency—they wanted variability.

Though routines, rituals, and solidified habits are essential to success, when your system wears you down, mixing things up is what creates progress and a greater sense of satisfaction. We all benefit greatly from seasons in our lives, variety in our projects, and a healthy swing of emotions. Living at the same pace every day is exhausting, no matter how fast or slow the speed actually appears to be.

When I think back on the best days of my life and the memories that stand out above others, I realize there is a not-so-subtle through-line. Each of these experiences involves me exerting extreme effort and/or celebrating an extreme effort. What now seems obvious in hindsight is that giving my all is deeply satisfying.

There's not much genuine joy in consuming endless hours of entertainment, day after day. It is highly unlikely that I will reflect back on my life many years from now and wish I had watched more television or played more video games. It just doesn't provide the beauty in life that I'm after.

Working hard is hard work, obviously. But working hard on something you care deeply about doesn't always feel hard. Instead, it can feel like the perfect way to spend a life of meaning, service, and achievement.

When paired with a grand celebration, working hard is somehow always worth it.

QUICK REVIEW: ADVANCED STRATEGIES

1. You don't have to implement every strategy in existence to get great results, but it's a good idea to see what opportunities exist that may take your health, growth, and productivity to the next level.

2. High achievers are always on the lookout for anything that will give them an extra edge because they know how valuable their time is to themselves and their success. Be ready and willing to try new things, even if they seem extreme, because that is where growth takes place—outside of your comfort zone.

3. Working hard on your goals is best countered by playing hard. The most satisfying days are often the ones where we give tremendous effort toward something we care deeply about, and then party like there's no tomorrow.

CHAPTER 10 ACTION PLAN

1. Schedule time on your calendar at least once a week to think. Write down an important and challenging question to answer. Then give yourself at least 20 to 30 minutes to brainstorm every possible answer.

The times each week you will block off for intentional thinking include:

The most important questions based on your quarterly grand goals that you want answers to are:

1) _____

2) _____

3) _____

2. Choose the best productivity music for your focused blocks of time. I recommend Focus@Will, but the best music for you is music that drowns out the noise of the world and allows you to dig in deep on your primary project.

The type of music or music service that you will be listening to while working includes:

_____

3. Build or buy a standing desk for use at home. If you are allowed, do so at the office as well.

The date you plan to research standing desks, standing mats, proper shoes, etc.:

_____

OR

The date you plan to research building your own standing desk:

_____

PART III:
THE 5 AM ACTION PLAN

CHAPTER 11
The 5 AM Action Plan

A 30-Day Program

Winners are wide awake; they are alive. Every day you
will find them in the marketplace making things happen.
The real winners are not just dreamers. Although they have
dreams, they are doers: They realize their dreams. They are
the bell ringers, always attempting to wake others up to the
numerous opportunities life offers.

—Bob Proctor, legendary personal
development author and speaker

Action is everything. It is the difference maker between success
and failure, achievement and regret, progress and stagnation.

Now that you have walked through all seven steps of The 5 AM
Blueprint, it's time to put those ideas into action. We discussed
many important concepts in the previous chapters, and I am certainly not expecting you to try everything right away.

The key is to focus on the vital few actions that will make the
biggest difference in your immediate future. Dominating your
day before breakfast is ultimately about focusing on your current
grandest goals.

What follows is a 30-day plan to implement the core strategies of The 5 AM Blueprint. This is your chance to pull out your

calendar and schedule the key activities that will get you from where you are to where you want to be.

30-DAY PLAN TO IMPLEMENT EVERYTHING

Day 1: Get Ready

- Finish reading this book from cover to cover.

- Review your notes, highlighted passages, and ideas scribbled in the margins. Identify which strategies stand out to you as ones you would like to begin immediately.

Day 2: Get Connected with Other Ambitious Early Risers

- Find a group near you that meets early in the morning, like a local running club, a business group that meets for breakfast, or schedule early morning activities with people you live with or near.

- Connect with others online in virtual groups, like Hal Elrod's Miracle Morning Community, Facebook.com/groups/MyTMMCommunity, or The 5 AM Miracle Community group on Facebook, Facebook.com/groups/The5AMMiracleCommunity/.

Day 3: Begin Your 5 AM Miracle

- Begin your transition to waking up a little earlier.

- Either set you alarm 15 minutes earlier than normal or prepare to wake up bright and early at your ideal time tomorrow morning.

Day 4: Create Your POP

- Design your Personal Optimization Plan, a set of circumstances when your life is working like a well-oiled machine.

- What does the highest and best version of yourself look like?

- What are you doing when everything is working well?

Day 5: Blueprint Step 1

- Brainstorm the list of your life's grandest goals.

- Feel free to think like a kid and fly to the moon. Be the fireman, princess, or astronaut you always knew you would be.

- What have you always wanted to do but never made time for?

Day 6: Blueprint Step 2

- Create your Quarter System.

- Choose the dates for your quarters (e.g. January to March) and clear your upcoming calendar.

- Choose your top two or three grandest goals to pursue this quarter and set up your goals notebook.

Day 7: Blueprint Step 3

- Clarify your daily anchor and complementary habits that are based on your grandest goals. The most common daily anchor habits include waking up early, working out, and beginning your day's work.

- Decide when each of your anchors will occur and which smaller habits will accompany them.

Day 8: Blueprint Step 4

- Create your ideal week template and create your ideal week.

- Be sure to include time for your ideal morning routine, ideal evening routine, and focused blocks of time for your current grand goals.

- Keep in mind that the goal is an *ideal* week, not a *perfect* week. Plan time to catch up when things don't go as planned.

Day 9: Ideal Morning

- Design your ideal morning routine.

- Plan your mornings backward from the time you begin work for the day to the time you wake up.

- Include time for your most critical anchor and complementary habits with a strong focus on energy and self-care.

Day 10: Ideal Evening

- Design your ideal evening routine.

- Plan your evenings backward from the time you fall asleep to the time you stop work for the day.

- Decide upon an evening boundary when your work will end and your routine begin.

Day 11: Blueprint Step 5

- Consolidate your tasks, projects, and events into a dedicated task manager. There are many great task managers to choose from and I have had great success with Nozbe.

- The key is to optimize the system by including every task, large and small, into one system so you are able to see everything in one location.

Day 12: Go Paperless

- Consolidate your documents, files, and folders into a digital filing service.

- Dropbox, Google Drive, Microsoft OneDrive, and Apple's iCloud Drive are all great choices to store your documents.

- It's best to choose one system for all of your items instead of spreading your data across multiple platforms.

Day 13: Get Evernote

- Consolidate your articles, notes, and ideas into a note-taking application.

- Evernote is the best choice for a digital system to store your note-related content.

Day 14: Get Focused

- Schedule focused, uninterrupted blocks of time onto your calendar for working on your grandest goals.

- Identify two to three locations where you can isolate yourself from people who may make you veer off course from your work.

- Get in the habit of turning off social media, mobile devices, and other potential distractions.

Day 15: Inbox Zero

- Clean up your emails to get to Inbox Zero.

- Plan a few days to play catch-up if your inbox is overflowing.

- Schedule time on your calendar to get back to zero emails at least once every 24 hours.

Day 16: Project Management Zero

- Complete any unfinished tasks to reach Project Management Zero.

- Take a detailed look at each of your projects and determine where you have loose ends and open loops.

- Schedule time at least once a week to rein in your projects and determine what your most important next actions will be.

Day 17: Desktop Zero

- Clear your desk to reach Desktop Zero.

- Get in the habit of only allowing materials on your desk that relate to your current task.

- Put everything away in a predetermined and organized location at the end of each day.

Day 18: Home Base Zero

- Clean up your home and office to reach Home Base Zero.

- Schedule time once a week to put everything away in its predetermined and organized location.

- Work toward the goal of putting everything away at least once a day.

Day 19: Blueprint Step 6

- Set up your Daily Rituals and Habits Tracker.

- Determine which daily habits are most important based on your current grand goals.

- Review your tracker during your weekly review.

Day 20: Weekly Review

- Set up your weekly review system.

- Schedule one or two hours per week, typically on Friday afternoon or Sunday evening, to review your past week and the week coming up.

- Determine what went well, what did not, and what changes you will make so the next week can be better than the last.

Day 21: Accountability Partner

- Connect with two to three people who could be your accountability partner.

- Set up an accountability system and meet with your partner on a recurring basis (e.g. weekly, biweekly, etc.).

- Align your accountability meetings with your weekly reviews to provide a solid context for your discussions.

Day 22: Monthly Review

- Set up your monthly review system.

- Schedule time at the end of each calendar month to review the previous weekly review documents.

- Review the progress you have made thus far on your current quarterly goals and determine what changes need to be made for the upcoming month.

Day 23: Quarterly Review

- Set up your quarterly review system.

- Schedule time at the end of each quarter to review the previous monthly review documents.

- Reflect on the achievement of your grandest goals and create your plan for the next quarter.

Day 24: Annual Review

- Set up your annual review system.

- Schedule time at the end of each calendar year to review the previous quarterly review documents.

- Reflect on the achievement of your grandest goals and determine what changes need to be made for the upcoming year.

Day 25: Blueprint Step 7

- Schedule a block of time (preferably up to an hour once a day) to think.

- Ask yourself a tough question based on your current quarterly goals and brainstorm the best possible answers.

Day 26: Listen Up

- Find your favorite productivity music.

- Focus on music that enhances your ability to think while avoiding distracting sounds.

- Sign up for Focus@Will to optimize your brain and productive time.

Day 27: Stand Up

- Enhance your daily productive flow with a standing desk.

- You can construct a very simple and effective standing desk with textbooks, cardboard boxes, or other easily available materials.

- Build or purchase a standing desk when you are ready to make a firm commitment.

Day 28: New Vision Board

- Create a vision board in your home or office.

- Using a corkboard or another similar surface, post images, quotations, and other visual reminders of the process to get to your grandest goals.

- Avoid using generic imagery of distant fantasies, and instead, focus on what you can do now to move the needle toward your current objectives.

Day 29: Hang Upside Down

- Research inversion, specifically what type of equipment you would like to purchase (gravity boots, inversion table, or inversion chair).

- Easily integrate inversion in your daily schedule by adding it as the last step to your exercise routine.

- Begin inverting for one minute and then build up to 10 or 15 minutes per session over the next few weeks.

Day 30: Connect in a Mastermind Group

- Find other ambitious, productive, and successful people who are pursuing goals similar to yours.

- Schedule time to meet, share ideas, and enhance each others' growth.

THE SUMMARY OF EVERYTHING: THE 5 AM MIRACLE IN THREE STEPS

I know that it can be daunting to even just glance at a list of 30 days' worth of actions. So here is the summary of everything in this book broken down into three simple steps—the same steps I previewed in the first chapter.

If you reach a panic point or you feel a bit overwhelmed, pause and refer back to these three steps.

1. Plan: Map out each day intentionally before it begins.

2. Execute: Make tangible progress through focused blocks of time on your grandest goals.

3. Review: Every week, fully review what you did and what you will do next.

Plan, execute, and review. That's it.

KILL THE SNOOZE BUTTON
Pitfalls, Mistakes, and Problems to Avoid

Domination is a daily decision.

It would be ideal if reading one great book, attending one inspiring conference, or talking to one fascinating person a single time was all it took to stay upbeat, positive, and motivated for life.

As it turns out, we need to be reenergized constantly. As Zig Ziglar, the late personal development legend, is known for saying, "People often say that motivation doesn't last. Well, neither does bathing—that's why we recommend it daily."

There are times when I lose my energy, feel down on myself, and begin to actually believe that my life is going nowhere. In these low moments it only takes a dash of brilliance to bring me back. When I know I'm in need of a pick-me-up, I turn on my favorite music and head out for a run, knowing that I can literally restart my life in that moment.

It's true that every day is the first day of the rest of your life, and if you want to begin again, all you have to do is take one simple action.

Tomorrow morning you have the opportunity to dominate your day. The best part is that you get that chance every single day for the rest of your life.

QUICK REVIEW: 30-DAY ACTION PLAN

1. It may be a bit ambitious to implement every strategy in this book, so be sure to identify the strategies that will have the biggest impact on your life in the near future.

2. You don't have to stick to a 30-day plan; however, it's best to set a firm deadline to hold yourself accountable as you implement the strategies you choose.

3. If you do nothing else, plan each day of your life with intention, purpose, and passion.

CHAPTER 11 ACTION PLAN

1. Since it's unrealistic to implement every idea, strategy, and tactic in this book at the same time, choose now which ones you want to pursue right away.

The most inspiring goals from this book that you want to pursue right away include:

1) _____

2) _____

3) _____

4) _____

5) _____

2. If you have not done so already, add your most important goals to your Quarter System for this quarter or the upcoming quarter.

The goals you will commit to for the upcoming quarter include:

1) _____

2) _____

3) _____

3. Using the 30-day template in the book, choose a starting date and then add each objective to your calendar or task manager. Alternatively, you can to sign up for the 30-day email reminder system at 5amBlueprint.com.

The date you will begin your 30-day challenge:

_____

CHAPTER 12

Time for Bold Action

Making Miracles Every Day

Don't ask for the task to be easy, just ask for it to be worth it. Don't wish it were easier, wish you were better. Don't ask for less challenge, ask for more skills. Don't ask for less problems, ask for more wisdom. It's the challenge that makes the experience.

—Jim Rohn, former author, speaker, and
personal development legend

In the first chapter, I asked you to make four ambitious commitments that would lay the foundation for achieving your own 5 a.m. miracle.

1. I will have an intentional and written plan for my day, every day.

2. I will consistently implement healthy habits for optimal energy and enthusiasm.

3. I will choose short-term objectives that help me achieve my life's grandest goals.

4. I will track my progress, make necessary adjustments, and hold myself accountable.

These are not easy commitments. They require consistent sacrifice, access to resources, and incredible patience as you make steady progress toward your grandest goals. The good news is that through the form of The 5 AM Blueprint, you now have the strategic game plan to make these commitments stick for life.

As with any worthy goal, long-term success is the pinnacle of achievement and that's what I hope for you. I firmly believe that if you follow the steps in this book, you can tangibly reach a level of achievement that previously may have only been a fantasy.

I know that's a bold statement and that's the point. Bold action is necessary for achieving grand goals and living a grand life.

Intentionally and consistently waking up early is a bold goal, and yet, it is only a small piece of a much larger puzzle. Following through on many well-chosen, high-impact, tiny daily decisions is the formula for crossing items off your list of grand goals.

Achieving your own 5 a.m. miracle is incredibly valuable— not because you wake up early to meditate or go for a run—but because the activities you choose each day will dictate everything about who you are and what you will have accomplished many years from now.

I hope you now see the beauty of what those tiny choices can mean for your future.

Every day matters.

Every beautiful, miraculous day.

As a final word, I want to whole-heartedly thank you for taking the time to read this book. It has been an honor to help you take your life to the next level and I can't wait to hear about all of your grand success!

Until next time, remember, *you have the power to change your life, and the fun begins bright and early!*

THE 5 AM TOOLBOX

The Top 10 Resources for 5 AM Pros

Here are the best resources to get fully connected and transition to the lifestyle of an intentionally ambitious early riser. I highly encourage you to plug in with others as you begin your journey, and these tools will provide the structure, support, and guidance for dominating your day before breakfast.

1. The 5 AM Studio: Exclusive Resources

This is the exclusive resource center for people just like you who have bought this book. In the studio, you can download step-by-step action plans to implement the core strategies of The 5 AM Blueprint.

JeffSanders.com/studio

2. The 5 AM Miracle Podcast: Weekly Inspiration

Every Monday morning I release a new podcast episode where I share a fascinating interview with an ambitious guest or I hop on the mic myself and discuss everything from early mornings and healthy habits to personal development and rockin' productivity.

5amMiraclePodcast.com

3. The 5 AM Club: Stay Up-to-Date

This is the best place to stay up-to-date with all of my latest blog posts, podcast episodes, exclusive discounts, and community announcements. It's free to sign up and you get free gifts!

JeffSanders.com/5amclub

4. The 5 AM Miracle Community: Get Connected

The community has grown over the last few years to become the premier place to connect with other ambitious early risers. Join the community for free today and start learning from seasoned 5:00 a.m. pros alongside newbies looking to learn more about what it means to dominate their day before breakfast.

JeffSanders.com/community

5. 47 Strategies: A Productivity Self-Assessment

If you are looking for a way to boost your productivity, this is a great place to start. The 47 Strategies Self-Assessment analyzes your current level of productivity and then offers advanced strategies to optimize your ability to get more done every day.

47Strategies.com

6. The 5 AM Affiliate Program: Sharing the 5 AM Message

If you have an audience that would benefit from their own 5 a.m. miracle, then I encourage you to sign up for my free affiliate program where you can earn hefty commissions for promoting 5 a.m. resources.

JeffSanders.com/affiliate

7. Additional Recommended Reading

Now that you have finished this book, here are a few phenomenal reads that will optimize your early-morning productivity.

1. *The ONE Thing* by Gary Keller and Jay Papasan

2. *Essentialism* by Greg McKeown

3. *The Compound Effect* by Darren Hardy

4. *The Miracle Morning* by Hal Elrod

5. *Getting Things Done* by David Allen

8. Submit Your 5 AM Success Story!

If you have seen great success in your own life because you implemented some of the strategies in this book, I want to hear about it! Just like my emails I will read every one that comes in, so don't be shy. Feel free to spill your guts and share your own 5 a.m. miracle!

JeffSanders.com/5amStory

AMBITIOUS ACTIONS LIST

Now that I have read this book, I will . . .

ACTION _____ DATE _____

1. _____ By _____

2. _____ By _____

3. _____ By _____

4. _____ By _____

5. _____ By _____

6. _____ By _____

7. _____ By _____

8. _____ By _____

9. _____ By _____

10. _____ By _____

11. _____ By _____

12. _____ By _____

13. _____ By _____

14. _____ By _____

15. _____ By _____

16. _____ By _____

17. _____ By _____

18. _____ By _____

19. _____ By _____

20. _____ By _____

References

Allen, David. *Getting Things Done*. New York: Penguin, 2002.

Auden, W. H. "The Life of That-There Poet." *New Yorker*, April 26, 1958.

"Benefits of Inversion." Teeter Hang Ups. Accessed July 2, 2015. www.teeter-inversion.com/Benefits-of-Inversion.

BusinessDictionary.com, s.v. "Parkinson's Law." Accessed July 2, 2015.http://www.businessdictionary.com/definition/Parkinson-s-Law.html

Carpenter, Sam. *Work the System*. 3rd ed. Austin: Greenleaf Book Group, 2011.

Clear, James. "How to Stop Procrastinating on Your Goals by Using the Seinfeld Strategy." Accessed June 30, 2015. www.jamesclear.com/stop-procrastinating-seinfeld-strategy.

Covey, Stephen. *The 7 Habits of Highly Effective People*. 6th ed. New York: Simon & Schuster, 2013.

Davis, Jim. *I'd Like Mornings if They Started Later*. Riverside: Andrews McMeel Publishing, 2013.

Duke University's Fuqua School of Business. "Apple CEO Tim Cook on Career Planning." YouTube video, 2:50. May 30, 2013. www.youtube.com/watch?v=a6g8y3EDHkw.

Einstein, Albert. Quoted in interview with John Archibald Wheeler, "From the Big Bang to the Big Crunch." By Mirjana R. Gearhart. *Cosmic Search* 1, no. 4 (Fall 1979).

Emerson, Ralph Waldo. *The Essays of Ralph Waldo Emerson*, edited by Alfred R. Ferguson, Jean Ferguson Carr, and Alfred Kazin. Cambridge: Belknap Press, 1987.

"Inversion Table Benefits." Best Inversion Table Reviews Guide. Accessed July 2, 2015. www.bestinversiontablereviews.com/top-12-inversion-table-benefits.

Johnson, Samuel. "The Vision of Theodore." In vol. 15 of *The Works of Samuel Johnson*, edited by Robert Lynam, 331-40. Troy: Pafraets Press, 1903.

Keller, Gary and Jay Papasan. *The ONE Thing*. Austin: Bard Press, 2013.

Lockhart, Robert. Absolute Abundance Raw Retreats. Accessed July 2, 2015. www.sunfoodhealthretreat.com.

Mann, Merlin. "Inbox Zero." 43 Folders. Last modified March 13, 2007. www.43folders.com/izero.

McKeown, Greg. *Essentialism*. New York: Crown Business, 2014.

Moran, Brian and Michael Lennington. *The 12-Week Year*. Hoboken: John Wiley & Sons, 2013.

Nightingale, Earl. *Lead the Field*. Wheeling: Nightingale-Conant, 1987. Audiobook, 6 compact discs; 5 hours.

Nisen, Max and Gus Lubin. "29 Successful People Who Wake Up Really Early." *Business Insider*. Last modified December 24, 2013. www.businessinsider. com/successful-people-who-wake-up-really-early-2013-12.

Ostrovsky, Larry and Oksana. "12 Health Benefits of Inversions." BeWellBuzz. Accessed July 2, 2015. www.bewellbuzz.com/wellness-buzz/inversions.

Oxford Dictionaries, s.v. "equilibrium." Accessed June 14, 2015. www.oxforddictionaries.com/us/definition/american_english/equilibrium.

Oxford Dictionaries, s.v. "miracle." Accessed March 17, 2015. www.oxforddictionaries.com/us/definition/american_english/miracle.

Proctor, Bob. *The ABCs of Success*. New York: Jeremy P. Tarcher, 2015.

Pressfield, Steven. *Turning Pro*. New York: Black Irish Entertainment, 2012.

Rohn, Jim. *The Treasury of Quotes*. Dalls: Jim Rohn International, 2006.

Skean, Wendy. "Face of the Race: Wendy Skean." By Leadville Race Series. Last modified February 23, 2015. www.leadvilleraceseries.com/2015/02/face-of-the-race-wendy-skean.

Sulzer, Jessica. "Brain Benefits of Inversion Tables." LiveStrong.com. Last Modified August 16, 2013. www.livestrong.com/article/359317-brain-benefits-of-inversion-tables.

"Viva Ned Flanders." *The Simpsons*. First broadcast January 10, 1999 by Fox. Directed by Neil Affleck and written by David M. Stern.

Williams, David. "Exercises to Help Drain Your Lymphatic System." Last modified June 29, 2015. www.drdavidwilliams.com/lymphatic-system-drainage-exercises.

Willingham, Tim. "Sitting Is Killing You." DailyInfographic. Last modified May 10, 2011. www.dailyinfographic.com/sitting-down-is-killing-you-infographic.

Ziglar, Zig. "Official Ziglar Quotes." Ziglar.com. Accessed June 19, 2015. www.ziglar.com/quotes/zig-ziglar/people-often-say-motivation-doesnt-last.

Acknowledgments

Publishing a book has been one of my life's grandest goals for nearly a decade. Though I did not initially think of myself as an author, after entering the world of personal development, I knew deep down that I wanted to model my life after the amazing men and women who have continually inspired me to become the highest and best version of myself.

When I sat down to write this section of the book, my wife, Tessa, challenged me to let go of my ego for a moment and truly acknowledge reality: Bringing this book to life has been nothing less than a community effort. Though my name is on the cover, it really should say, "Created by the 5 a.m. miracle global community, an ambitious group of early risers who want nothing more than extraordinary achievement."

I need accountability and motivation just as much as anyone, and this book has been a phenomenal test of endurance, discipline, and prioritization. To that end, I want to thank every single person who has helped contribute to this book's fruition.

First, I want to thank God. A major part of my own morning routine is reading the Bible and spending a few moments in prayer. My mornings have become my best chance to deepen my faith and reconnect with what matters most in my life. To that end, this work would not be possible without a few real miracles and I never give Him enough credit for those.

To my wife, Tessa. Without you this book would not exist. You have worked tirelessly to keep our lives moving forward as I have been the wild card, trying to build a business and pursue endless crazy ideas. You are my biggest cheerleader and always hold me to a high level of excellence, even when I want to cut corners. I can't thank you enough and I will love you always!

To my endlessly quirky pug, Benny. You are the mascot of my podcast and the only soul who has heard me record every episode. I don't think you did much to help make this book happen (after all, you did take a lot of naps during work hours), but you are really funny and a great companion. Thanks for being a man's best friend.

To my family, especially my parents, Brian and Loretta, and my brother, Tim, you have never ceased supporting me through my wild ambitions and that means everything to me. Even when it appears that I am heading off the deep end, you stand by and help me with unconditional love. That's all a grateful son and brother could ever ask for. Big thanks to the rest of my awesome family, Diana and Marc Olive, Janet and Ken Meyer, Helen and Raymond Sapp, Dorothy and Milt Sanders, and Mary and Leon Hoskins. I love you all!

To my friend and weekly accountability partner, Matt Frazier. You have been a guiding light and inspiration to me for years. Thank you for keeping me on my toes and sharing so much of your life, business, and wisdom with me. It's ambitious people like you that remind me to keep pushing the boundaries of what's possible.

To my incredibly generous attorney and talented friend, Andrea Wallace. You went above and beyond helping me with contract negotiations and navigating the crazy legal jungle that only you know so well. Next time I will actually pay you, I promise.

To my lifelong friends going all the way back to early childhood, especially Pearce Landry-Wegener, Tyler Mallory, Jesse McIntosh, Andrea Wallace, Megan Fox, Juliette Schmidt, and Peter Curby, you guys are my rock. You have seen me at my best and certainly at my worst. Thank you for putting up with me through it all. I love you guys!

To my friends, coworkers, and leaders at Anthem, especially Rachel Chandler, Michael Harlan, Sarah Fossett, Bailey McChesney, Chris Perry, Mark Roberts, Karen Pitts, Samantha Cox, and Ryan Ball, thank you for standing beside me through the formative years of my blog and podcast. Whether you realize it or not, you helped create this and I wouldn't be where I am today without you.

To my fellow Nashville podcasters, especially Jeff Brown, David Hooper, Dave Kirby, and Stu Gray, thank you for letting me sit and absorb your collective radio genius. It's a little daunting to be surrounded by such talent and it's humbling to know how much further I have to go. Thank you for paving the way and making this job look so easy.

To my mentors, including the authors, speakers, coaches, podcasters, bloggers, designers, online marketers, and content creators who have been pushing the envelope for years ahead of me, thank you for doing the hard work so I wouldn't have to. Without you I would still be where I was years ago, *graduated and clueless*. I want to personally thank Michael Hyatt, Darren Hardy, David Allen, Rich Roll, Erik Fisher, Hal Elrod, Bob Proctor, Dan Miller, Nicole Antoinette, Dean Karnazes, Grant Baldwin, Jess Lively, Sean Stephenson, August Turak, Todd Henry, Jeff Goins, and Ray Edwards for exemplifying an authentically great life and purposeful business.

To my publishing team at Ulysses Press, especially my editor Kelly Reed, you gave me my first chance to publish a book professionally and that is a real testament of your faith in me. Thank you for this amazing opportunity to share my thoughts with the world. I will be forever grateful.

At its core, this book is a comprehensive manifestation of my blog and podcast. The readers of my articles and the listeners of my show embody the spirit of *The 5 AM Miracle* more than anyone and they are my constant source of inspiration. To all of my fans around the globe, it has been an honor creating content each and every week for you and I thank you for making this book possible. You rock!

About the Author

Jeff Sanders is a productivity coach, plant-based ultramarathon runner, and host of The 5 AM Miracle podcast. He has a bachelor of arts degree in Theatre and Psychology from Truman State University and lives in Nashville with his lovely wife Tessa and quirky pug Benny. To learn more about Jeff and how you can dominate your day before breakfast, visit JeffSanders.com.

***

As you begin to experience your own 5:00 a.m. miracle, I highly encourage you to share your journey with this hashtag: #5amMiracle.

If you follow the hashtag on Twitter, you can connect with others as they begin their early-morning miracle right alongside you.

If you want to connect with me directly, you can explore my website, JeffSanders.com; find me on Twitter, @JeffSandersTV; friend me on Facebook, JeffSanders.com/facebook; and even send me an email, Jeff@JeffSanders.com.